An Incautious Man

LIVES OF THE FOUNDERS

EDITED BY JOSIAH BUNTING III

ALSO IN SERIES:

FORGOTTEN FOUNDER, DRUNKEN PROPHET:
THE LIFE OF LUTHER MARTIN
Bill Kauffman

AN INCAUTIOUS MAN

THE LIFE OF GOUVERNEUR MORRIS

Melanie Randolph Miller

ISI
BOOKS

WILMINGTON, DELAWARE

Miller, Melanie Randolph, 1953–

    An incautious man : the life of Gouverneur Morris / Melanie Miller.— 1st ed.—Wilmington, Del. : ISI Books, c2008.

        p. ; cm.
        (Lives of the founders)

        ISBN: 978-1-933859-72-9
        Includes bibliographical references and index.

        1. Morris, Gouverneur, 1752–1816. 2. United States—Politics and government—1775–1783. 3. United States—Politics and government—1783–1789. I. Title. II. Life of Gouverneur Morris.

E302.6.M7 M55 2008   2008928377
973.3/0924—dc22   0809

ISI Books
Intercollegiate Studies Institute
Post Office Box 4431
Wilmington, DE 19807-0431
www.isibooks.org   ·

Manufactured in the United States of America

This book is dedicated to my husband,
David Michael Archung, with love.

CONTENTS

LIST OF ILLUSTRATIONS

Fig. 5: *Independence Hall, the site of the Constitutional Convention of 1787, where Morris gave some of the most eloquent speeches that were heard that summer and wrote the Constitution's final draft.* Independence Hall, Philadelphia, courtesy Corbis.

Fig. 6: *The U.S. Constitution, with Morris's powerful words of introduction: "We the People of the United States." By using these words instead of a list of the thirteen states, Morris's masterful editing forced the document to transcend state identities and speak for all Americans.* Courtesy of the U.S. National Archives.

Fig. 7: *A page from the volume of Morris's Paris diary at the Library of Congress, showing the beginning of the entry of the fateful day of August 10, 1792, when the Tuileries Palace was attacked and King Louis XVI fell. "The Cannon begin and Musquetry mingled with them announce a warm Day," Morris recorded.* Courtesy of Library of Congress national manuscript collection.

Fig. 8: *Gouverneur Morris by Ezra Ames. This is a late portrait of Morris, dating from around 1815, a year before his death at the age of sixty-four.* Collection of the New-York Historical Society, Accession Number: 1817.1.

ACKNOWLEDGMENTS

I WOULD LIKE TO THANK MY FATHER, ROBERT DEMOREST Miller, for his unfaltering support in this project and in all other aspects of my life; my friends and former professors Peter P. Hill and Richard Stott for their unstinting encouragement of and help with my work; and William Howard Adams and Richard Brookhiser, two fellow Morrisophiles who have done much to increase public appreciation of this worthy man.

A note on the text: quoted passages from Morris and others appear as transcribed in the editions of the primary sources cited in the bibliography. Readers should be aware that Morris followed the common eighteenth-century convention of capitalizing most nouns, often used "it's" for the possessive, utilized multiple variations in spelling, and generally avoided commas. Even so, I have chosen not to insert "[sic]" where Morris's spelling and usage deviates from current practice.

Fig. 1: *Gouverneur Morris in 1779, twenty-seven years old and in the Continental Congress; a 1783 engraving by Benoit Louis Prevost of a drawing from the life by Eugène Du Simitière.*

INTRODUCTION

"I AM NOT A CAUTIOUS MAN"*

WE AMERICANS ENJOY READING ABOUT OUR FOUNDING Fathers partly as an exercise in self-congratulation—they are in our blood, their accomplishments "belong" to us, and because of their achievements we feel a natural superiority to every other nation. True, our Founders had faults, and we occasionally examine those faults with an uneasy feeling, wary that their flaws will diminish our confidence in their stature and, with it, the stature of our nation. Nevertheless, the Founders have for the most part survived these periodic acid baths of criticism to remain monumental in our minds.

Yet there is at least one Founding Father who has never formed a significant part of these self-congratulatory meditations: Gouverneur Morris. This fact has many causes, including Morris's own indifference to the judgments of his contemporaries and posterity.

---

* Gouverneur Morris to William Short, September 18, 1790.

Yet Morris was important. The greatest injustice done to Morris has long been—and, at the hands of many historians continues to be—dismissal of him as a "lightweight." It's an injustice he would have undoubtedly ignored, but it nevertheless obstructs a proper recognition and appreciation of what Morris did for America. The dismissal of Morris has discouraged the sort of study of his writings and life that, in the case of Jefferson, Washington, Hamilton, and Madison, has so enriched American history. This is too bad, for the study of Morris has a great deal to offer those interested in diplomacy, politics, law, race relations, gender studies, and other fields of inquiry. Similarly, Morris's contribution to the success of the American Revolution has been underappreciated, as has been his critical work on the U.S. Constitution and his time as Jefferson's successor as minister to France during the French Revolution.

Morris could write with great eloquence and beauty. He was exceptionally funny and loved to laugh, and his humor runs like quicksilver throughout his diaries, letters, speeches, and the few surviving firsthand accounts of Morris in action. There is no doubt that his friend, the supposedly somber George Washington, savored Morris's tremendous sense of fun. At the same time, Washington perceived and valued his other talents. Morris could produce, at lightning speed, complex planning documents incorporating a range of policy concerns—for so one might describe the hundreds of bills and public statements he wrote for the New York Provincial Congress, the Continental Congress, and the Constitutional Convention. He had the ability to debate thoroughly and confidently in a way that assured that issues were fully examined, from the speeches he delivered on the floor of Congress to the receiving-room diplomatic battles he waged with the best of the English Foreign Office. Washington also knew that Morris was no idealist, that his reports on any subject were not colored with romanticism but rather showed real understanding. The president could also rely on Morris's strong sense of duty to his country, a loyalty that led him to stay in France as minister through a nightmarish time that we—despite our ample modern experience with anarchy and terrorism—still perhaps have not really comprehended.

Yet Gouverneur Morris continues to resist absorption into the Founding Fathers Club, that little group of wise men we like to imagine perched on a heavenly cloud, watching and protecting our country. Perhaps the greatest count against him from a historian's point of view was his persistently Federalist view. The consensus is one of disapproval of the Federalist party, which dwindled throughout the early 1800s, even as the Republicans dismantled the country's navy and army and parried ineffectively with the sophisticated and merciless foreign policy of Britain and France. Moreover, in opposing the War of 1812, Morris sacrificed much of his patriotic reputation in advocating a separation of North and South in order to allow the North to stay out of the conflict. Though Morris was passionate in his love of America and his outrage over what was, in his view, a war resulting from gross incompetence and immoral motives, the faint tinge of "traitor" seems to hang about him in his last years and has helped to push him off the stage.

Finally, Morris's reputation has suffered because he was unpopular with some of the other Founding Fathers. John Adams did not think much of him, and the feeling was mutual. The prim New Englander's views may have reflected disdain for Morris's effervescence and supposedly immoral ways more than a rejection of his work as a public servant; and the fact that Adams's son-in-law was at one time in direct competition with Morris for a diplomatic position likely did not help. Jefferson liked Morris, but their budding friendship in Paris was blighted by years of mudslinging at Morris by Jefferson's friends, and their views on the French Revolution diverged so drastically after Jefferson returned to America that friendship between the two was for many years impossible. Moreover, Morris's scorn for most of Jefferson's (and Madison's) actions as president was undoubtedly known to the thin-skinned Virginian. Communication between the two men near the end of their lives, however, indicates that they retained a genuine feeling of regard for each other.

In sum, Morris is worth knowing better, much better than we have known him heretofore. This book seeks to present Gouverneur Morris to the modern American reader who is interested in the Founding generation and who will welcome in his imagination the company of a sophisticated, compassionate, energetic man whose loss of a leg at the age of twenty-eight did nothing to diminish his enjoyment of life or his service to his country. Morris's was a full, difficult, but happy life, and, though he never thought of it in such a way, it was a gift to the nation.

CHAPTER ONE

A NEW YORK BIRTHRIGHT

The Just the righteous man is brave
Nor to himselfe nor none a Slave
The giddy mob his Soull disdaines
The frownes of tyrants he contemns
Firme to his purpose bravely Stands
Unmovd by their unjust commands

—Lewis Morris, grandfather of
Gouverneur Morris, c. 1708

GOUVERNEUR MORRIS WAS THE SCION OF A REMARKABLE
New York family that, from the moment of its arrival in New York,
displayed the leaping ambition, intelligence, and nerve necessary to
succeed in the grasping free-for-all that typified the colony during
late-Dutch and early-English control. The prizes for good political
connections were rich—land and social standing—and Morris's

great-great-uncle and great-grandfather were able to break in to the highest echelons of the colony, improving their family's position and fortunes significantly.

Morris's great-grandfather, Richard Morris, and Richard's brother, Lewis, were Welshmen who had served in Oliver Cromwell's armies. They had settled in Barbados sometime around the 1640s and had prospered there, but the prospects must have appeared even brighter in New York after the British took over from the Dutch. In 1668, Richard went to New York with his wife, where they acquired a large tract of land in what would one day be known as the Bronx, ten miles north of Manhattan; the tract and their residence became known as Morrisania. The Morrises lived there only a few years, however, dying within a short time of each other in 1672, and survived only by their son Lewis, Gouverneur's grandfather, who was less than a year old.

The elder Lewis (now seventy-two) promptly came to take charge of his nephew and namesake and the family's property. Lewis's business ability showed no decrease with age, and during the two decades he lived in New York he expanded the family holdings to over nine thousand acres in New York and New Jersey. He was less successful with his strong-willed nephew. When he was sixteen, the younger Lewis apparently defied his uncle and left New York for adventures in Virginia and Jamaica, returning home just before his uncle's death in 1691 at the remarkable age of ninety-one. The elder Lewis was not pleased with the miscreant, and his will contains a sharp rebuke of his heir for his "great Miscarriages and Disobedience." Nonetheless, his uncle died childless, and the younger Morris was a wealthy man at the age of twenty.

Lewis seems to have inherited a double measure of ambition and ability from his two remarkable forbears. His talents were reflected not only in increased property but in accession of political power, which began during the year of his inheritance when he married Isabella Graham, the daughter of the New York attorney general. It was a happy marriage, producing twelve surviving children. In 1692, Morris was appointed to the Governor's Council of New York, and in 1715 he became the first supreme court justice for the colony, a post he held for nearly twenty years. He rounded off his career with the governorship of New Jersey in 1738.

Lewis Morris apparently felt no need to embrace convention in his pursuit of these prizes. He was a self-educated man whose intellectual appetite led him to compile one of the largest private libraries in the New World, second only to Harvard's. He reveled in political confrontation, even writing poetry about it. His most significant altercation was with colonial New York governor William Cosby, a brawling dispute that culminated in the famous trial of John Peter Zenger, a printer who, at Morris's bidding, had published a fulminating denunciation of the luckless Cosby. When Zenger was acquitted of libel charges, the triumph resonated with the issue of freedom of the press under the British constitution. Cosby's defeat in court was a point of pride with the Morris family, and Gouverneur would later describe it as "the Morningstar of American freedom," an attractive description that ignores the self-interested political maneuvering by his grandfather, and the fact that once he became governor of New Jersey Lewis Morris kept a firm grip on power and opposed any attempt by the Assembly to challenge his authority. Nonetheless, the basic tenet behind Lewis Morris's objection to Cosby—that incompetence and corruption were a legitimate basis to demand a governor's removal, even though colonial governors were appointed by the king—was an important element of the political philosophy that eventually would lead Americans to frame the American constitution, as important as the right to pillory an official in the press.

Gouverneur's father was Lewis's eldest son, Lewis Jr., born in 1698. He was a lawyer, and participated in his fair share of his father's political scraps, including the Zenger case. After the successful face-off with Cosby, Lewis Jr. was rewarded with the prestigious position of judge of the vice admiralty court of New York, with a jurisdiction that also included New Jersey and Connecticut. He apparently did not significantly enhance his inheritance, which included Morrisania, but this may have been affected by the fact that his first wife died when he was thirty-two, leaving him with four young children to raise. He did not marry again until shortly after his father's death in 1746; perhaps he had wished to avoid the disapproval of his strong-willed elder.

His new wife, Sarah Gouverneur, who was sixteen years younger than Lewis, also came from notable New York stock. Gouverneur's mother was clearly a strong personality who could endure much. When her husband died in 1762, she was forty-seven, with five young children, unfriendly adult stepchildren, and a significant estate to manage. She would later resist the decisions of three of her stepchildren and three of her own children to join the Americans against the British, creating a family schism that must have been painful to her. Though she stayed in Morrisania, behind British lines, during the war, her loyalty was rewarded with the exploitation by both sides of the assets of the estate—including the razing of its valuable rich timber for firewood for British troops, and the loss of the family's beloved library. She died in 1786, at the age of seventy-one, not long after the war ended.

Lewis Morris Jr.'s tenure as judge both reflected and perpetuated the family's substantial social position in the colony, and

Fig. 2: Morrisania, where Morris was born and where he died. The ancestral mansion in the Bronx was in disrepair when Morris returned from Paris, and he proceeded to rebuild it and furnish it with the acquisitions he had made in Paris. It was torn down in 1905.

Gouverneur, who was born on January 30, 1752, would be very conscious of that status as he grew up. Yet it may not have been as important to his father: when Lewis wrote his will in 1760, he displayed the self-deprecating and wry humor that his father's will had also exhibited, and that Gouverneur would perfect. "My Actions," he wrote, "have been so inconsiderable in the World that the Most durable Monument will but perpetuate my folly while it lasts." His desire, therefore, was that "nothing be mentioned about me, not so much as a line in a News Paper to tell the World I am dead." "That I have lived to very little purpose my Children will remember with concern when they see the small Pittance I have left them, for Children judge of the Wisdom Goodness and *affec-*

tions of their Parents by the Largeness of the bequests coming to them but what I have left them is honestly acquired, which gives me a satisfaction that Ill got thousands cannot bestow."

More seriously, however, he lamented the hostility of his older children to his second wife and their five children. He told his stepchildren that Sarah had done them "equal justice" with her own, and that they should be dutiful to her. He had already given a major part of the estate to his eldest son, Lewis Morris the third. The rest, including the manor house, was given to Sarah with a life interest, to go to his second son, Staats Morris, on her death. Gouverneur was to get two thousand pounds, and each daughter six hundred.

Lewis's will also directed that Gouverneur receive the "best Education that is to be had in Europe or America," with the interesting exception of Connecticut (that is, Yale), "Lest he should imbibe" that "low craft and cunning so incident to the People of that Colony, which is so interwoven in their Constitutions." This oddly vituperative injunction probably arose from the fact that at the time Lewis wrote the will, New York was in the throes of an extraordinary political dispute between the Anglicans (generally Tory) and the Presbyterians (generally Whig) for control of the newly chartered King's College (later Columbia University). The principal opponents of Anglican control were graduates of Yale. As his older sons had attended Yale, Lewis Morris's criticism hints at a significant dispute of some sort between the father and those sons, a dispute that was perhaps related to this issue.

The provision in the will regarding Gouverneur's education was also proof that the judge's youngest son—his only son with Sarah—though only eight when the document was written, had already demonstrated remarkable intelligence. While still quite young, he had been sent to learn French from a Swiss reverend in the nearby Huguenot village of New Rochelle, gaining a facility that would serve him well in his career. When he was nine years old, his father enrolled him in the Academy of Philadelphia. The academy had been founded in 1751 with an emphasis on the principles of education espoused by Benjamin Franklin, but by Gouverneur's time the curriculum stressed the classics and Latin rather than the more pragmatic subjects—math, geometry, and English—favored by Franklin. While in Philadelphia, Gouverneur lived with his half-sister, Mary Morris (twenty-eight years his senior) and her husband. The years in Philadelphia must have given the young Gouverneur a sense of the greater world and its possibilities, for it was then the largest and most sophisticated city in America, second in size only to London in the British Empire.

Gouverneur had been at the school for only a year when word came in July 1762 of his father's death. It must have been a bad blow, but Gouverneur would emerge into young manhood with apparently unshakable optimism and a great gift for enjoying life. There may have been indirect effects from the loss of his father, however, ones with profound consequences: despite his Whig connections, it seems highly likely that Judge Morris, had he lived, would have stayed with his wife on the side of the crown when the Revolution came, and whether Gouverneur would have defied his father is impossible to say. (He did defy his mother.) Moreover, Gouverneur did not have a chance really to absorb or admire his parents' apparent devotion to each other. For this reason, perhaps, he would long declare his determination to be a "confirmed Bachelor" and often wrote in his diary of the fleeting and unreliable nature of the love of men and women for each other and the inevitable disappointment of marriage.

In 1764, while his widowed mother was grappling with management of the Morrisania estate, Gouverneur entered King's College. At age twelve, three years younger than his classmates, Gouverneur was one of eight in his year; by the time he graduated, the class had dwindled to five.

The sectarian conflict sparked by the establishment of King's College had not abated, although the issue of the school's charter had been settled in 1753 by a compromise that gave the Anglicans control of the school but put half of the public money collected for its establishment toward a new pesthouse and jail. (One Whig opponent of the college expressed pleasure that at least the money was to be "divided between the two pesthouses.")

The King's College curriculum, like that of the Academy of Philadelphia, was largely classical, emphasizing "logic, rhetoric, metaphysics, ethics, English verses and essays, and 'moral philosophy,'" with some work in government and international law. The regime was rigorous: students rose at five in the morning to go to prayer, attended classes until six in the evening, and went to bed at nine.

All was not study and prayer at school, however, as the school's records show. In a vain effort to pen the energetic young men inside the school compound, the trustees at one point authorized erection of an eight-foot fence with nails protruding from the top. In the spring of 1766, a fourteen-year-old Gouverneur and some of his older friends scandalized the school with an assault on the character of one of their tutors, Robert Harpur. He was Irish, which may have contributed to the prejudice against him, and was apparently overly strict. The students posted a scurrilous cartoon of Harpur, alleging that he had seduced a young woman and then, when she got pregnant, paid for an abortion. The school investigated, and, finding insufficient proof of the allegations, suspended one of the boys and publicly admonished the others, including Gouverneur.

Gouverneur's time at the school was interrupted in August 1766 when his right forearm was badly scalded by a kettle of boiling water. The extremely painful injury apparently left the flesh on his arm scarred and wasted, and he stayed at home to recover for almost a year afterward. This incident and the resulting disfiguration must have been profoundly distressing for a teenager, but little or no word of it appears in his personal papers, and the only evidence that it occurred and caused permanent damage is in the writings of others. He must have worked on his studies while at home, for when he returned to King's College he quickly caught up with his class.

In 1768, the sixteen-year-old Gouverneur graduated and began his training as an attorney in the prosperous law offices of an old family friend, William Smith Jr., whose father had been a close associate of Gouverneur's grandfather. The profession was a natural choice for Gouverneur, given his father's and grandfather's legal careers and the fact that his half-brother Richard was now a judge. The bar rules required three years of clerking, rather than a formal legal education, and much of the training was via the tedious labor of copying laws, briefs, titles, filings, and correspondence. Gouverneur emerged from it not only with a grounding in the law but also with the ability to write for hours at a time in an excellent hand, a skill he would employ for the rest of his life. While he wrote, he was able to listen in on the animated discussions of the others in the firm.

William Smith Jr. was a man of great intellectual energy that extended well beyond the demands of his practice. He and one of his partners, William Livingston, had been two of the three prin-

cipal Yale-educated apostates (the "triumvirate") who had so force-
fully objected to the Anglican control of publicly funded King's
College. Their campaign, which had enlisted the support of the
lower classes of the city, had roiled the political waters of mid-cen-
tury New York. Their strategy would backfire, at least in Smith's
view, for the strong response of the artisan classes helped to create
the impetus for the Sons of Liberty movement and the shift toward
broad defiance of the crown.

Smith was a scholar who had published a highly respected history of the colony of New York. Perhaps encouraged by Smith,
Gouverneur continued at King's College while clerking and in
1771, at age nineteen, received a master's degree. He had discovered a considerable talent for the study of economics and finance,
quickly absorbing the arcane principles involved and their practical application. In 1770 he published an anonymous petition at-
tacking a New York assembly proposal to issue loan certificates.
The petition was sophisticated in reasoning and impressive in its
calculations, and when Gouverneur was revealed as its author he
was thereafter an acknowledged expert in the field.

In October 1771, Morris took the oath and entered the bar,
but he was restless, and less than a year later he considered leaving
America for a year in England, hoping to obtain a European gloss
and refinement that he believed would be an advantage in America.
He proposed the trip to Smith, his mentor of the past several years,
telling him that he felt he "been so hurried through the different
scenes of childhood and youth, that I have still some time left to
pause before I tread the great stage of life." He did not mention
another motive: during the previous autumn, he had fallen in love
with Kitty Livingston, one of the great New York Livingston clan
and the daughter of Smith's former law partner. Though he sent

her letters about his attachment over the next year—"I certainly dream of nothing else," he wrote her in the summer of 1772—by early 1773 he had given up his suit.

Smith promptly advised Morris against the trip to England. Making money first, he said, was critical; "both virtue and ambition abhor poverty, or they are mad." Sounding much like Polonious counseling Hamlet, he advised Morris to imitate his extremely successful grandfather, Lewis Sr., who "sought preferment *here* and built upon his American stock." (Interestingly, Smith made no mention of Gouverneur's father as a model.) He closed by deferring to Gouverneur's mother, who would have to underwrite such a trip; perhaps she objected, or Gouverneur simply thought the better of it, for he did not go.

Instead, he devoted himself to his legal work. The results, in the first years of the 1770s, were promising. His half-brother Richard gave him business, and he handled cases relating to Morrisania on his mother's behalf. Friends also gave him work, and he was able to charge substantial fees. His cases ran the gamut from election challenges to commercial transactions.

He also entered into the pleasures of New York society with all the boundless energy that a young man in his early twenties, though working very long hours and "up all night writing," can invest. So-called "social clubs" were a principal means of entertainment. Morris joined one that counted many of his friends among its members, often attending what he described as "balls, concerts, and assemblies—all of us mad in the pursuit of pleasure."

He must have been a center of attention. The painting by Charles Wilson Peale, made when he was thirty, is the only one we have of Morris in his youth that is lifelike, and it shows a striking and graceful young man—he was over six feet tall—with a strong nose, beautifully arched dark eyebrows over thoughtful hazel eyes, and lips twisting in humor. It is evident from his features that Morris was someone who smiled a great deal, an impression confirmed by his friends' accounts.

Morris's clubs and the need to establish himself financially absorbed his entire attention in this period, but while he filed court papers and wrote briefs and danced, the American Revolution was bearing down on him, his colleagues, and his friends. It would soon sweep them up and scatter them; in some cases, as with William Smith Jr., it would tear them away from their previous lives and connections for good. Still others, like Morris, would hesitate before finally leaping into the conflict on the side of the Revolution. In so doing, they would assist its success both as a military effort and as a political metamorphosis.

CHAPTER TWO

A VERNAL MORNING

THE SIGNS OF TROUBLE, OF COURSE, HAD BEEN THERE FOR some time. The first phase of the revolutionary crisis began in 1763, at the end of the Seven Years War, when Gouverneur was eleven. The war had been very expensive for the mother country—many believed England had achieved victory over the French simply by pouring more money into it—and most people in Britain agreed that the colonists should help repay those costs and cover the heavy outlay occasioned by the decision to post twenty British battalions in the Americas on a permanent footing. The means of collection was to be through enforcement of the longstanding Navigation Acts, the foundation of the British mercantile system, a system of government-imposed monopolies that had actually largely benefited the colonies by squelching competition from other countries.

The 1764 Sugar Act imposed rigorous measures to ensure collection of already required customs on certain shipments. The regulations were enforced off the coast by British naval vessels and affected even intercolonial shipments, to the outrage of the colonists. Next came the Currency Act, prohibiting the specie-poor colonies from printing paper money and thus damaging the ability of American merchants to get commercial credit. Finally, in 1765, the most notorious of the revenue measures was enacted: the Stamp Act, which taxed just about every item of paper with writing on it: newspapers, legal documents, even tax receipts. This act challenged the colonists' belief that they had the sole right to impose such direct internal taxes, but their London agents lobbied against it in vain. Parliament passed the Stamp Act with what was noted to be "less opposition than a turnpike bill."

The colonists did not submit to the Stamp Act but rather "stood Bluff." The Virginia House of Burgesses, ever jealous of what it saw as its taxing prerogatives, passed the Stamp Act Resolves, which asserted their exclusive right to impose taxes. In Boston, the stamp distributor was threatened and resigned, and the other colonies followed suit so that by November only Georgia had not forced its distributor out. In October 1765, the Stamp Act Congress, consisting of delegates from nine colonies, met in New York and passed resolutions against the act.

Secret societies composed of artisans and tradesmen and opposed to the Stamp Act began to form. Called "the Sons of Liberty" after a phrase used by a sympathetic British member of Parliament to describe Americans, these groups tried various means to provoke opposition to Parliament. Some of their efforts were peaceful, even occasionally silly, but others amounted to outright lawlessness. An angry theatergoer recorded one incident in New York City in 1766:

> This evening a play was acted by permission of our Governor, to
> be performed by a company of comedians or Strollers, notwith-
> standing the Sons of Liberty without any Reason given pulled
> down the Playhouse the beginning of the 2nd act, put out all the
> lights, then began picking of pockets, stealing watches, throw-
> ing brick Bats, sticks and bottles and glasses, crying out Liberty,
> Liberty, then proceeded to the Fields or Common and burnt the
> materials. One boy Killed and Many people hurt in this Licen-
> tious affair.

Gouverneur may well have witnessed this uproar firsthand. Epi-
sodes such as these gave the New York elite a reasonable fear of
mobs, a fear that would militate against the move to revolution
nine years later.

Nonetheless, opposition to the Stamp Act was virtually unanimous, and the taxes couldn't be collected. It was repealed in 1766,
though primarily due to the complaints of unhappy British merchants. William Pitt, who had strongly opposed the Stamp Act,
returned as prime minister, but his poor health kept him from
being effective, and King George III was able to push through a
number of the most offensive measures, which in the end led to
war. In 1767, New York was the target of the Townshend Acts,
which ordered the New York assembly to provide supplies for British troops in America and, until it did so, declared the assembly
suspended. The act also created duties on new items, including tea
and blank writing paper.

In Boston, where customs officers took advantage of the new
rules to create what has been called a system of "customs racketeer-
ing" at the expense of the colonists, a boycott was organized in
October 1767, and in early 1768 Samuel Adams and his fellow Sons

of Liberty sent a circular letter to the other colonies asking them to join together to oppose the acts. Boycotts of British goods were organized in Boston, New York, and Philadelphia.

In late 1768, two British regiments arrived in Boston to keep the peace, adding to American fears of forcible subjugation. The tension in that city, tight as a violin string, snapped with the Boston Massacre in March 1770, just one month before the Townshend Acts were repealed. With the orderly administration of the trial of the British soldiers, however, the British government was reassured that the rule of law was still respected in America, and matters remained reasonably quiet for the next two years. Nonetheless, "committees of correspondence" were formed in towns throughout the colonies and began to communicate with each other at the colony level, one of the first steps in forming what would later be the revolutionary government. They were ready when thirty-seven-year-old Lord North became the new prime minister and took the fateful step of granting the struggling East India Company a virtual monopoly on tea shipped to America through a government rebate on the customs duty. Colonial leaders in the port cities agreed that ships carrying such tea would not be allowed to land or to pay the duty, and in December 1773 the leaders in Massachusetts, now known as Patriots, threw 342 chests of tea into Boston harbor.

Gouverneur Morris appears to have been detached from the approaching storm, distracted by work and social activities. In January 1774, now twenty-two years old, he wrote to a friend in Pennsylvania complaining of angst about politics, love, and religion. That year he joined the elite Moot Club, becoming one of twenty members of the cream of New York's legal profession. Without a doubt, the Moot members, who met regularly at the historic King's Tavern, discussed the state of affairs with England. They would soon be forced to move past discussion and choose sides: in April 1774, the New York Sons of Liberty followed the example of their Boston brothers and held their own tea party in New York harbor. The act alarmed the more conservative residents of the city, and when news came a few weeks later that the British were closing and blockading Boston harbor and that the New York Sons of Liberty were going to call for an embargo on all imports in a show of solidarity, the well-to-do attempted to take control of events. At a public meeting called by the Sons of Liberty to appoint a committee to organize the embargo, the merchants gained agreement to expand the committee's size and include members from their own rank. The result was a half-radical, half-cautious body called the "Committee of Fifty-One," and it included many of Morris's friends.

It is not surprising that Morris and others like him initially urged that the only realistic avenue for the colonists was to reach an agreement with Britain, providing for "[i]nternal taxation to be left with ourselves. The right of regulating trade to be vested in Britain, where alone is found the power of protecting it." After attending the meeting in late May at which the committee nominations were confirmed by the people, Morris wrote a letter about his doubts about the ability of the two groups—whom he called "the people of property" and "the tradesmen"—to work together successfully. Morris, who had faith in neither group, gave an analysis of the situation remarkably similar to what he would say of the elite instigators of the French Revolution fifteen years later: he saw that the bourgeoisie had used the poorer classes to oppose the British, stirring them up so that they "roared out liberty, and property and religion," but that the "sheep" had begun to produce their own shepherds:

The mob begins to think and to reason. Poor reptiles! It is for them a vernal morning, they are struggling to cast off their winter's slough, they bask in the sunshine, and ere noon they will bite, depend on it. The gentry begin to fear this. Their committee will be appointed, they will deceive the people, and again forfeit a share of their confidence. And if these instances of what with one side is policy, with the other perfidy, shall continue to increase, and become more frequent, farewell aristocracy. I see, and I see it with fear and trembling, that if the disputes with Britain continue, we shall be under the worst of all possible dominions. We shall be under the domination of a riotous mob.

These unguarded comments have been used by historians to label Morris as an aristocrat who despised the less fortunate and uneducated, and who was alarmed at the thought that they might take control. Yet the letter shows that Morris was clear-eyed about the vulnerability of the uneducated lower classes to manipulation by the upper classes, and that he believed that the fissure with England opened two possibilities, neither good: "domination of a riotous mob," which history indicated would lead to anarchy and eventually despotism, as the people would eventually turn to anyone who would restore order; or an oligarchy of the rich. It would take a war in which the upper and lower classes had to cooperate and trust each other to help produce the intellectual evolution of the next decade and to reach the concept that a government could be successfully designed that would protect the vulnerable and limit the power of the rich and well born.

The march toward revolution continued. When the First Continental Congress was convened in Philadelphia in September 1774, New York sent delegates chosen by a combination of the Committee of Fifty-One and other New York committees. In mid-September, Paul Revere galloped from Boston to Philadelphia with a copy of the inflammatory Suffolk Resolves, declaring that George III was the sovereign only by the will of the people, and proposing civil disobedience to royal administration, military preparation, and commercial protest. On September 17, a divided Congress passed the Resolves and established the "Continental Association," which placed an immediate ban on British tea, with other goods to follow starting in December, and discouraged consumption of British articles already in the colonies. Local enforcement committees would be created, and all individuals were required to take an oath to uphold the association, creating yet another means of political participation for men of lower social status. In New York City, the association was enthusiastically enforced.

Parliament reacted to the sharp drop in trade in early 1775 with the punitive New England Restraining Act (soon extended down the coast), which restricted colonial ships from the North Atlantic fisheries and limited colonial trade to England only. The British administration also sent orders to General Gage to seize American arms stored at Concord, leading to the historic clashes on April 19 at Lexington and Concord between American Minutemen and British troops. News of the battles and of the Restraining Act led the colonists to call the Second Continental Congress in May. In New York, the Committee of Sixty, successor to the Committee of Fifty-One, called for a provincial assembly or congress that would assume responsibility for governing New York and send delegates to the Continental Congress. At a public meeting attended by over eight thousand people, New Yorkers agreed to obey the directions of the committee rather than those of the royal colonial assembly. Oaths were to be sworn by every citizen, a strict measure that put the better-known dissenting residents at the mercy of suspicious crowds.

The very foundations of New York society were cracking underfoot, and the lines of division cut right through the middle of the Morris family. Gouverneur's brother-in-law Isaac Wilkins was an outspoken opponent of the new order; he would later move to Nova Scotia. His other brothers-in-law were firmly on the Patriot side, for when a vote was taken in Westchester County to appoint the new assembly, the victors included Gouverneur and his brother Lewis. The new body set to work to obtain armaments and shore up defenses while the British were evacuating Manhattan. The evacuation involved the departure of the remaining British garrison to a warship in the harbor. Many Patriots assumed that they were on their way to help subdue Boston and therefore demanded that their supplies be forcibly appropriated. Morris disagreed. War had not yet been declared, and he feared that snatching British arms or abusing British troops could lead to an explosion in a city not yet prepared for war. Morris persuaded the Provincial Congress to issue orders against any interference with the departure of the British, and to a large extent these measures were obeyed.

Yet clashes were inevitable, and in early June 1775, Morris was in a crowd watching the garrison on its way to the harbor when the reins of the lead horse were snatched by a man named Marinus Willett, who was determined to prevent the loss of the supplies. Willett knew who Morris was and was astounded when the young man stepped forward and objected to his actions as a violation of the Provincial Congress's orders. John Morin Scott, Morris's Moot colleague, now a zealot in the committee governing the city, was in the crowd. He contradicted Morris, giving the unnerved Willett the chance to lead off the supply carts and leave the troops to board the ships empty-handed. However, Morris persevered and quickly obtained a vote from the Provincial Congress asserting its authority as superior to that of the New York committee, and ordering the restoration of the arms to the crown. The episode demonstrated Morris's lifelong determination to insist on the rational pursuit of aims by exercise of government authority rather than by the fleeting, if satisfying, power of the mob.

The fact that Morris was now a full participant in a revolutionary government, even though he still hoped for reconciliation, indicates that at some point during the previous year his political views had altered significantly.* Joining the revolt entailed the obvious risk of emotional and material devastation, and in the case of Morris the emotional impact was immediate, for his mother chose the British side, as did two of his sisters and some of his close friends. Yet he did not falter. That a majority of the colonists decided to take their chances against the enormous power of Britain when they might lose everything, including their lives—and that they would be joined by Morris, who, as a young unmarried man had less to lose than many but was still going far beyond anything his father or grandfather, with their crown-appointed positions, ever could have imagined or condoned—is one of the extraordinary ponderables of the American Revolution.

---

* William Howard Adams notes that it is "impossible to identify a moment of epiphany" for Morris, but that it had certainly taken place by the time of his election to the new assembly.

CHAPTER THREE

"THIS IS THE SEED TIME OF
GLORY AS OF FREEDOM"*

GOUVERNEUR MORRIS'S BRILLIANCE, FUELED BY HIS YOUTH, would be a significant asset to the revolutionary cause. This brilliance first became evident in the workings of the new and unsteady New York Provincial Congress when the question of financing the war preparations grew critical. Morris quickly produced a remarkable document recommending that the Continental Congress issue a currency, with each colony assigned a share of the debt. The benefit of a single currency in promoting the union of the colonies was implicit in his thinking, and when he presented the plan to an audience consisting of the Provincial Congress and established local merchants, the approval was unanimous and the plan was endorsed by the Continental Congress as well.

---

* Morris, at Valley Forge, to Robert R. Livingston, February 22, 1778

The Provincial Congress had not yet given up hope for accommodation, and when Morris drafted its instructions to the Philadelphia delegates he included a statement urging them to "use every Effort for the compromising of this unnatural Quarrel between the Parent and the Child," because "contests for Liberty, fostered in their Infancy by the virtuous and wise, become Sources of Power to wicked and designing Men [and] . . . frequently end in the Demolition of those Rights and Privileges, which they were instituted to defend." Morris was only twenty-three when he wrote these powerful words. With such demonstrations of talent, it is no surprise that New Yorkers (and later the Continental Congress) came to rely heavily on his extraordinary ability to analyze and to write.

They relied on Morris for more than that. On June 25, 1775, in a fascinating bit of theater, the royal governor of New York returned from England, landing in New York harbor. On the same date the newly appointed commander-in-chief, George Washington, was scheduled to pass through the city on his way to Boston. Morris, who was on the ceremonial committee, arranged for Washington's enthusiastic welcome at 4 p.m., complete with a parade. It was the first meeting for Morris and Washington, and Morris would come to admire Washington enormously. Four hours after Washington's fête, the royal governor was greeted by a far more sedate ceremonial group that included royal officials of the colony and members of the Provincial Congress, Morris among them.

During the summer of 1775, while the first battles with the British were fought in and around Boston, the New York Provincial Congress tried to find its way in handling its many new responsibilities. Morris worked at a terrific rate, attending meetings and helping implement measures. The city's economy staggered as many left, and the effects of the nonimportation policy began to be severe. The news that England was preparing for war frightened many in the Provincial Congress away from attending sessions. The government's paralysis in the face of increasing danger led to a call for new elections in November, but the new body—to which Morris was not elected—was also impotent, and it foundered in only six weeks. The third congress, which included Morris, might have suffered the same fate but for news of the king's angry declaration that nothing but complete submission by the colonists would be accepted, an ultimatum that stiffened the Americans' resolve as no internal appeal had been able to do. For many, including Morris, the news from England that their former government had ordered them cut off and would block all trade was decisive: from now on, the only goal was independence.

As it became clear that the dispute would now move to the battlefield, Morris, along with many patricians with no military experience, applied for an officer's commission. The Provincial Congress refused to endorse their applications to the Continental Congress, in the case of Morris recommending instead an experienced militiaman with the humble trade of shoemaker. Morris was chagrined at this denial of something to which he clearly felt his social rank entitled him. He complained to his brother Lewis of his dismay that "a herd of Mechanicks are preferred before the best Families in the Colony." His prejudices, along with those of his friends, would be challenged and forcibly altered by a war where for sheer survival the rebelling colonies would have to rely on those citizens with military talent and experience rather than social rank. Morris would remain a civilian, concluding that his "little Abilities were more adapted to the Deliberations of the Cabinet than the glorious Labours of the Field."

During the term of the third Provincial Congress, Morris persuaded his colleagues that it was time to draft a constitution for a new government of New York—and to elect a fourth Congress to do it. His speech, given in May 1776, was a tour de force, and his arguments in the ensuing debate won the day. He pointed out that the fundamental powers of a new government had already been exercised by the provincial congresses—"coining money, raising armies, regulating commerce, peace, war, all these things you are not only adepts in, but masters of"—and that a functioning revolutionary government was clearly possible. He did not speak merely of New York, however. His vision was wider and it was prophetic. Indeed, for a twenty-four-year-old who had only joined the revolt a year earlier, it was extraordinary. Morris foresaw a single national congress, elected by small districts, with three-year term limits; the elimination of boundaries between the colonies; and the prosperity of a new America that would be "an Asylum from Oppression" to all who came there.

With Morris's prodding, New York was ready to cross the Rubicon. On July 9, 1776, the day it first convened, the fourth Provincial Congress, again including Morris, agreed without dissent to authorize its delegates to the Continental Congress to ratify the Declaration of Independence.

Meanwhile, the early maneuvers of the war continued. Washington had returned to New York in mid-April to face an anticipated attack by Lord Howe on the city. Morris was appointed to a committee to coordinate with Washington in efforts to oust suspected Tories and make an example of them. The committee's actions, endorsed by Washington, appear to have been effective but do not make pleasant reading. Morris himself suggested that a Loyalist steward at the Livingston Manor estate near New York

City who was attempting to sign up the manor's tenants to the Tory side should be hanged in front of those tenants because "nothing but ocular Demonstrations can convince these incredulous Beings that we really do hang them." The suggestion was followed, and Livingston Manor quickly met its quota in enlistments for the Revolutionary Army.

Morris's membership on the committee also put him in the position of judging the fate of his family's old friend, his former employer William Smith Jr. Though he had consistently and trenchantly criticized Parliament's intrusions into the colonial establishment, Smith was unwilling to let those objections rise to the level of justifying revolt. He had successfully claimed neutrality, but by summer 1776 this was no longer acceptable, and he was called by the committee to explain his position or face arrest. He told the committee that he believed America and Britain would still reconcile, and that he could not "suppress the Convictions of my own Mind." Morris wrote to his old friend that he personally did not accept Smith's "neutral" position, for his countrymen needed Smith's abilities in their cause, and such efforts would be rewarded in the new order that would follow. A year later, the committee sent Smith on parole to Livingston Manor; he finally declared for the British and was permitted to go behind British lines, eventually leaving for England. He would end up the chief justice of Canada.

Morris's friend Peter Van Schaack, who had clerked with him at Smith's office, was also unable to bring himself to the revolutionary side and in 1778 was exiled to England. He would return after the war. Morris wrote him an affectionate farewell:

> I would to God that every tear could be wiped away from every eye. But so long as there are Men so long it will and must happen that they must minister to the miseries of each other. It is a

delightful object in history to see order and peace and happiness result from confusion and war and distress. It is a pleasing hope of life. It is your misfortune to be one of the many who have suffered. In your philosophy in yourself in the consciousness of acting as you think right you are to seek consolation while you shape your old course in a country new.

In August 1776, the hopes of the Patriots received a serious setback when Washington lost the Battle of Long Island and the British returned with a vengeance to take New York City, where they would stay for the duration of the war. Morrisania was over-run by British troops; Morris heard little of his mother except, in December, the terrible news that one of his sisters had died. His letter of condolence to Sarah was sympathetic but may well have offended her, for, like any young political zealot, Morris called on her to acknowledge that the current struggle for the happiness of the many meant "we soon feel the insignificancy of the individual." This was hardly likely to console someone who had lost a child, not to mention someone on the Loyalist side; perhaps it was meant to excuse his failure to come to Sarah's assistance when he was instead devoting himself to the needs of the revolutionary cause. He would later attempt to visit her behind enemy lines, but in the face of the suspicion this aroused concerning his loyalties, he renounced the effort.

In late September 1776, the British entered New York City. Within a week, fires were started that destroyed a quarter of the city, including King's College. Washington and his troops retreat-ed, and the Provincial Congress moved up the Hudson to Fishkill. It lacked enough members to meet, so a Committee of Safety was created to handle affairs. Morris, who was in New Jersey with his sister Euphemia, was among the missing. He did not return to the Congress until the end of November, and he offered no explanation to his outraged colleagues other than that there had been a "Series of Accidents too trifling for recital." The real reason behind his supposed dalliance in New Jersey remains uncertain, but the language is similar to the language Morris would later use when he had been ill. Whatever the reasons for his absence, Morris plunged back into the work of the Congress at Fishkill, serving on committees and drafting official letters and reports at blinding speed. His work was conducted in the face of bad news from the war front: by February, the British successes again forced the New York Congress up the Hudson, to Kingston.

Morris's immediate assignment at Kingston was to deliberate on the new constitution for New York. His views on the proper scope and authority of such documents were already well formed. Unlike Jefferson, Morris did not believe that governments ought to be premised on the "natural rights" of man: to the pragmatic Morris, that seductive phrase simply meant doing as one wished without regard to the consequences for others. Meaningful rights were, rather, those rights "necessary for the preservation of society"—that is, property rights and political liberty (the right to participate in government and to hold it accountable).

The structure needed to establish and enforce such rights was debated throughout the chilly spring of 1777 in a foul-smelling room above the local jail in Kingston. Morris supported a strong executive, but the other members were in no mood to welcome a powerful governor like the royal ones of the past, and when he moved that the governor should have a qualified veto and total power over appointments, his motions were soundly rejected. He also moved that the convention "earnestly" recommend to future assemblies the abolition of slavery, acknowledging that it would not be feasible in the midst of war to take this step. This, too, was voted down. He had more success in defeating a measure advanced by John Jay to keep Catholics out of government. However, he was unable to stop another anti-Catholic measure pushed by Jay, one that prohibited the naturalization of Catholics unless they renounced "all allegiance and subjection" to the pope.

The proposed constitution, largely drafted by Jay but amended during the spring of 1777 on the floor of the congress (a process that gave Morris valuable experience for the federal convention ten years later), was adopted by a near-unanimous vote, and new state officials were quickly appointed. Morris refused all appointments, but he did agree to serve on an interim administrative Committee of Safety until a governor, senate, and assembly were elected.

While the new government struggled to its feet, New York was in mortal peril from the British, who were pursuing a three-pronged approach to dividing New England from the rest of the colonies. Sir William Howe, now in control of New York City, was to move toward Albany and meet with General Burgoyne, coming down from Canada and across from Lake Champlain to the Hudson, and with St. Leger, who was to arrive through the Mohawk Valley.

Things went as planned for the British—at first. Burgoyne and his eight thousand troops bested General Arthur St. Clair at Ticonderoga and forced his troops across Lake Champlain in early June 1777. This was a major blow to the Americans, and the New York Committee of Safety promptly sent Morris and another member to look into the defeat. The summer travel was slow, and they did not arrive at Fort Edward until the middle of July, where they conferred with generals St. Clair and Philip Schuyler. Perhaps influenced by his difficult trip, Morris suggested the strategy that would ultimately prevail against the British: "if we lay it down as a maxim, never to contend for ground but in the last necessity, and to leave nothing but a wilderness to the enemy, their progress must be impeded by obstacles which it is not in human nature to surmount." He also reported to the committee on the apathy of the nearby counties and their failure to provide soldiers for the effort, and he noted British efforts to beguile Vermonters with the promise that they would become a separate province.

The report, though frank and informative, was not what the committee had wished. The defeat at Ticonderoga had been demoralizing and they had wanted Morris to provide optimistic propaganda. Morris received a rebuke drafted by his old friend Robert R. Livingston, who said, "We are silent because we have nothing to say; and the people suspect the worst, because we say nothing." Angered by the complaint, the two men wrote back that they had not thought they were supposed simply to "write the news," a response that further irritated the committee, which recalled the two men. When Morris returned he gave a thorough report of the situation and the desperate need for reinforcements for the outnumbered Schuyler, and the committee agreed to let him go to General Washington to make the request.

On July 29, Morris and John Jay left for Pennsylvania to find Washington, who was hoping to stop Howe from taking Philadelphia. Washington could not spare any troops, so they went on to Philadelphia to petition the Continental Congress. On arrival, they learned that the Congress had replaced the able Schuyler with the ambitious Horatio Gates. Armed with additional news of potential calamity near Albany, Morris and Jay persuaded Congress to send five hundred riflemen as reinforcements. Those riflemen, under Daniel Morgan, would prove vital in the upcoming battle of Saratoga.

Morris returned to New York on August 20 and found that the situation was increasingly grave. Sir Henry Clinton, rather than William Howe, who was now in Philadelphia, had begun the British push up the Hudson to Albany for his rendezvous with Burgoyne. However, Clinton would not complete that rendezvous: news came of the British disaster at the second battle of Saratoga in mid-October, and the situation, politically and militarily, was radically changed.

Despite the encouraging news, Kingston had to be evacuated, for the British came through in mid-October. Morris, who had a wagon and horses, helped with the withdrawal, as did other members of the legislature.

A few days later, Morris departed for the Continental Congress, which had fled from Philadelphia to York, but he would not arrive for nearly three months, once again staying at his sister's home in New Jersey, apparently, and once again with no explanation for his delay.

Upon arriving in York, Morris was almost immediately sent to Valley Forge to consult with Washington about the army's supply organization; it was the disgraceful failure to deliver, rather than an inadequate supply of provisions, that had put the men at Valley Forge in terrible straits the previous winter. Profiteering at the expense of the army—through the selling of supplies to the cash-paying British—was rampant. Morris promptly began an assessment of the complex and inadequate system. His committee ordered inventories, drafted new rules, and queried the colonies about making greater contributions of provisions.

Morris's committee was also assigned to coordinate with Washington on a plan to rid the army of incompetent officers, change the army's regulations, "and adopt such other measures as they shall judge necessary for introducing economy and promoting discipline and good morals in the army." Shortly after arriving at Valley Forge, they sent a letter to Congress recommending appointment of Philip Schuyler as the new quartermaster general. The recommendation was ignored, but Congress's preferred candidate, the able Nathanael Greene, was appointed, and Morris and Greene became friends.

The committee was also instructed to address the sad state of military morale. The available instruments included pay incentives; reorganization of the army's basic units of infantry, artillery, engineers, and cavalry; and recruitment initiatives, which included drafting men from the state militias. Washington's recommendations on these matters were sent to York, and when Morris returned there he made himself the primary advocate for adoption of the measures. Congress adopted the crucial changes to regimental organization but attempted to duck Washington's strongest recommendation, half-pay for life for officers, by sending it to the colonies for consideration, a move that would have scuttled it. This effort was defeated by a whisker when Morris, counting the votes, sent an urgent plea to Robert Morris of Pennsylvania—"Think one Moment and come here the next"—to swing the Pennsylvania delegation against it.

Morris's review of the army's supply situation necessitated an examination of the underlying finances, and after his return to York he prepared a detailed and remarkable document titled *Proposal to congress Concerning Management of the Debt—Finance, Army, Supplies, etc.,* premised on the need to consolidate the states' debt into

Fig. 3: A painting dated 1783 of Gouverneur Morris (seated) and his friend, the financier Robert Morris, by Charles Wilson Peale. Gouverneur's humorous affability and striking looks are apparent in this portrait.

the hands of the national government. Each state would abolish its separate currency and exchange it for continental certificates, a move that would stabilize the country's currency. In order to put critically needed funds into the national treasury, Morris proposed a loan be obtained in Europe, secured by public lands; states would turn over their western lands to Congress in exchange for paying down their share of the joint debt. National tariffs would be imposed to assure national revenue. He recommended that a treasury board be established to administer these steps.

He also sketched out the design of a strong centralized government, with a chief executive or committee, and other executive committees below to handle the different issues of the war effort—naval affairs, commercial affairs, and the army supply system. As an earlier biographer of Morris's role in the Revolution, Max Mintz, has noted, "The striking feature of this paper was not only that it constituted a comprehensive design by a young man of twenty-six to promote essentially a centralized government—a plan ten years ahead of its time—but also that its author single-handedly managed to carry all its provisions to the floor of Congress for consideration." His recommendation for a treasury board was passed in late September. His remaining proposals failed. It would take ten years of weak central government and its pernicious consequences to convince his listeners that a strong federal government was essential to the survival of the new nation.

CHAPTER FOUR

THE ACCIDENT

AT ABOUT THE SAME TIME THAT GOUVERNEUR MORRIS WAS drafting his financial proposals, the war was entering a new phase with the entry of a new combatant—France, whose decision to join the Americans was in large part due to the resounding American victory over an entire British army at Saratoga in the fall of 1777. The loss unnerved the British government (George III reportedly "fell into agonies" at the news), and the French recognized that a turning point had been reached.

The Americans knew something was in the air when they learned that Parliament had appointed commissioners, led by the Earl of Carlisle, to negotiate with the Americans and offer the right of taxing themselves. To those familiar with Realpolitik, including Gouverneur Morris, this was a clear indication that Britain was not simply thinking the better of its actions but was uneasy about something else; and on May 2, 1778, that something else was confirmed with the arrival of news that treaties of alliance and commerce had been concluded with France.

Yet Congress feared that the British commissioners could seriously undercut the people's resolve to continue fighting, and Morris was given the job of publishing an address warning Americans against trusting the British or accepting anything short of independence. This address did not include Morris's usual elegant rhetoric. It sounded more like something from the pulpit of a radical minister. "Arise then! To your tents!" Morris trumpeted. The British had "filled up the measure of their abominations, and like ripe fruit must soon drop from the tree."

The reception of the Carlisle Commission was accordingly cold; or rather, there was no reception at all. After much debate over whether the full proposal should even be given the dignity of being read in Congress, a committee was named—as always, including Morris—to compose the stinging reply. "Nothing but an earnest desire to spare the further effusion of human blood could have induced" Congress to read the proposal, "or to consider propositions so derogatory to the honor of an independent nation." This was Morris's language, and he supplemented it with anonymous letters to the *Pennsylvania Gazette* to make it very clear to the commissioners that the colonial relationship was over.

A week after the Carlisle proposal was received, Congress learned that the British had evacuated Philadelphia. They had—relatively speaking—enjoyed their stay. General Howe had made a local contractor's wife his mistress, and the many Loyalists in the city had lavishly entertained the British officers. It had been a great deal more comfortable there for the British than it would have been to fight with Washington on the bleak winter landscape of Valley Forge. (Benjamin Franklin responded to an inquiry about whether Howe had taken Philadelphia with the riposte that "in truth, Philadelphia has taken Howe.") Howe's displeased superiors sent Sir Henry Clinton to replace him, but Clinton's mission became one of evacuation in order to avoid a confrontation with the French fleet, which they knew as early as January 1778 was on its way to Delaware Bay. Washington followed Clinton, and on June 28 he provoked the inconclusive Battle of Monmouth, the last action that was to be fought by the two main armies of the British and Americans.

Though the British chose not to burn Philadelphia, they left it a shambles. Congress could not convene for several weeks in its old quarters at the Pennsylvania House ("Independence Hall") because of the stench from a nearby pit of dead horses and men. Basements had been converted to privies, flies swarmed everywhere, and as many as six hundred houses had been destroyed. Morris, with his occasionally overblown youthful zeal, suggested to Washington that the inhabitants who had remained during the British occupation should be subject to an enormous fine and remain under arrest until it was paid. It is surprising that the overtaxed Washington even bothered to reply to such a wild suggestion, but he courteously and firmly told Morris that such an "arbitrary stretch of power would inflame the country as well as city and lay the foundation of much evil."

The French fleet arrived in early July, along with the new minister plenipotentiary to America, Alexandre Gérard. Gérard's arrival marked the first official mission from one of the great European powers, and Congress scurried to prepare an appropriately dignified official welcome. Morris, of course, was on the committee. The diplomatic niceties of the era might seem trite today, but prestige could at that time be measured in the height of a man's chair on a stage, and which side made the first bows, and Morris was determined that the new nation should not embarrass itself. Logically, therefore, he and the other Americans consulted with Gérard himself, and on August 6, 1778, the first American state reception took place, a stiff but successful ceremony.

With a new and powerful ally, Congress began to draft instructions for America's new minister to France, Benjamin Franklin. Morris was on the committee and communicated regularly with Gérard concerning the work, giving the diplomat unusual influence, but Congress knew that French cooperation was paramount, and Gérard's input was considered vital. The instructions described the absolute necessity of obtaining loans from France to keep the war going. Morris prepared an accompanying paper titled *Observations on the Finances of America*. This document would considerably impress the French, whose own finances would soon teeter on the brink of collapse.

The entry of France into the war, which raised the chances of success but also brought the inescapable difficulties of administering an alliance, turned out to be a catalyst for some of the ugliest infighting Congress had yet seen. At the center of the brawl were the ill-fated Silas Deane, his disgruntled fellow commissioner to Paris, Arthur Lee, and Thomas Paine, whose ability with a pen had garnered him the position of clerk of the Committee of Secret Correspondence (which handled foreign affairs). Deane, a Connecticut businessman and friend of John Jay, had been sent to then neutral France in 1776 on a secret mission to obtain munitions and other military supplies. He was also an excellent military recruiter, and his efforts procured the invaluable assistance of the Baron von Steuben and the Marquis de Lafayette, among others. He worked with Pierre Augustin de Beaumarchais, one of

Louis XVI's secret agents, and procured several shiploads of supplies for America.

Deane was joined in late 1776 by Arthur Lee and Benjamin Franklin as commissioners to the court of France. Lee and Deane detested each other, and their antagonism festered to the point that Lee accused Deane of profiteering, which led to Deane's recall to America to face charges concerning the materials furnished by Beaumarchais. Deane claimed that they had resulted from a commercial transaction requiring payment to Beaumarchais and a commission to Deane, and were not an outright gift from the French king. When Deane published a defense on the subject in November 1778, Paine, who believed Arthur Lee, published a series of articles in rebuttal, citing secret documents concerning French-American relations prior to 1778, documents accessible to him only by virtue of his position as clerk of the Committee of Secret Correspondence. Paine's action outraged Gérard because France had been officially neutral at the time the supplies were provided.

The sides taken were a harbinger of the party lines that would emerge in the 1790s, with the more democratic and idealistic (including New England "radicals" as well as many southerners) siding with Lee, and Deane supported by the men Max Mintz describes as of a "cosmopolitan cast of mind, alive to the emerging position of the United States in a world of nations." Gérard demanded Paine's dismissal. On January 9, 1779, after a heated debate—in which Morris delivered a fiery speech that damned Paine and demanded he be dismissed without a hearing—Congress voted to require Paine's resignation. While Morris's object may have been valid, for Paine's actions were dangerously indiscreet, Morris's description of Paine as a "meer Adventurer from England, without Fortune, without Family or Connections, ignorant even of Grammar" did him little credit. Paine was thin-skinned, and when he was shown a copy of the proceedings the same night, Morris's comments were surely burned into his memory. His future conduct toward Morris would reveal calculated, if concealed, dislike. But Morris was not one to hold a grudge, and it was characteristic of him that twelve years later, in friendly conversation with Paine in Paris, he did not hesitate to "frankly acknowledge that I urged his Dismission from the Office."

With the instructions sent to the commissioners in Paris, Gérard requested a statement of war aims from Congress. This was a seemingly straightforward request, but the undertaking roiled the congressional waters and again exposed serious divisions that would continue to plague the new nation. Morris was named to chair the five-man committee to consider the matter. On February 23, the report came to the floor. In addition to British recognition of American independence, the committee recommended that Congress should instruct the commissioners to demand acknowledgment of the new nation's boundaries of the Mississippi River to the west, Canada to the north, and Florida to the south, as well as total evacuation of British forces from America's territories and waters and the provision of access to a port at the mouth of the Mississippi River. There were secondary items that the committee suggested could be negotiated: claims to Nova Scotia, in exchange for fishing rights off Newfoundland, renunciation of territorial expansion, and cession of the Floridas to Spain. The other members of Congress, however, had different ideas, depending on their regions: the southerners were adamant about free navigation and a port on the Mississippi. The New England states were unyielding on the fishing rights. It took six months of debate before the New England members would concur with a report stating that the fisheries were "of the utmost importance," but that this condition was not an ultimatum for purposes of a peace treaty. The southern states eventually agreed that if Spain became an American ally America could offer her the Floridas in return for navigation rights on the Mississippi; as Spain never allied with America, this last hope expired.

The unceasing demands made on Morris took a considerable toll. He complained to a friend that his constant work meant that he could take no exercise other than walking from "where I now sit about fifty yards to Congress" and back. He was also facing financial hardship because of the war-inflated costs of living in Philadelphia. "In times like the present I dare not, I cannot quit my post though to continue at it is big with ruin. Should I leave the State unrepresented I shall be censured by all," he wrote.

Yet for all of his efforts for the nation as a whole, and despite the heavy reliance Congress placed on him, his home state was not so happy, for many there believed he was putting the national interest ahead of New York's. Much of the dissatisfaction had to do with his perceived unwillingness to advance New York's claims to the areas that would become Vermont against both the claims of New Hampshire and the territory's demand to become its own state. Morris did what he could, though he was skeptical of the advisability and justice of the effort. His constituents believed him insufficiently aggressive, and in October 1779 he was defeated in the election for another term in Congress. Though there were many who disliked his style in Congress, most acknowledged that they were losing an invaluable workhorse. John Jay, who was fond of Morris even though his exuberance often dismayed the older and more sober statesman, wrote from Spain to George Clinton that it was "a Pity that one so capable of serving his Country should be unemployed, but there are men who fear and envy his Talents and take ungenerous advantage of his Foibles."

Morris was philosophical about the defeat and probably even relieved to give up the burden of office, though he stayed and worked until his replacement arrived in mid-November 1779. He also was waiting to see if a nomination as secretary to Franklin in Paris would come through. His opponents, who were many, need not have worried, because the accident that deprived Morris of his left leg also removed him from the field for the post of secretary.

There are slightly differing accounts of this tragedy, but probably the most reliable, one which apparently has not been previously published, is that written by William Churchill Houston to Phillip Schuyler on the day following the accident:

> I am unhappy this Morning to inform you of an Accident which happened yesterday to Mr. Gouverneur Morris. He was riding out in a Phaeton, and the Horses taking a Fright ran away in the Street, struck the Carriage against a Post, broke it all to Pieces and in the Shock fractured Mr. Morris's Ancle to such a Degree that it became necessary to take off his Leg imediately. He bore the Operation with amazing Firmness. I have not seen him but am told this morning, that though his Fever is pretty high and he has a good Deal of Pain he is not in Danger of Life. The Bruises he received in the Fall are a great Addition to the principal Accident. There was no Person with him in the Carriage.*

It is uncertain whether the recommendation to amputate, made by the attending doctors—who did not include his usual

---

* William Churchill Houston wrote this letter to Phillip Schuyler on May 15, 1780.

Fig. 4: Morris's wooden leg, now in the collection of the New York Historical Society. He lost his leg due to a carriage accident in May 1780, and over the years would suffer from inflammations and spasms in the stump, but he would continue to walk miles at a time until his death and never complained of it.

physician, his old friend Samuel Jones, who was out of town—was a sound one. Jones himself would later disagree with it; but it was too late, and Morris suffered his loss "with becoming fortitude," according to his close friend Robert R. Livingston. There was no anesthesia, of course, and no painkillers for the recuperative period. At the time, only about one-third of those who underwent amputation survived the surgery and resulting shock, which sends the body temperature plummeting. Morris, fortunately, was young and strong.

Morris's ability to ride a horse and his athleticism and mobility were permanently curtailed, and gout, the hideously painful bane of the Morris family, came to him perhaps sooner and more harshly because of his decreased mobility. Yet anyone who reads his papers is hard put to find evidence of his handicap; though he may well have endured phantom limb pain, a common side effect of amputation, his diaries rarely mention physical discomfort. As a pragmatist, Morris may have found comfort in the awareness that his disability was not unusual in a day when amputations were a common treatment for multiple fractures, infections, and battle wounds.

Nonetheless, Morris's ordeal deserves to be acknowledged. It was the second time he had been badly hurt and suffered great pain. The first time was at age fourteen, when he was severely burned; and now to be crippled at age twenty-eight must have been a terrible blow. Trials such as these can be fatal to a person's character—or they can strengthen it. Morris, clearly in the latter category, was able to treat the loss with detached good humor. One famous anecdote retold many years later is so typical of Morris that, although some historians regard it as hearsay, it seems likely to be true: after listening to various visitors and doctors admire the neatness with which the amputation had been performed, he said, "You speak so eloquently, would it not be advantageous to remove the other limb? We might then have a brace."

The accident also made Morris vulnerable to love, and, unsurprisingly, he fell in love with the woman who nursed him throughout his recovery. Elizabeth Plater was the wife of his friend George Plater, a member of Congress who would eventually be the sixth governor of Maryland. According to a French officer serving in America, Mrs. Plater was "typical of Philadelphia's charming women; her taste is as delicate as her health: an enthusiast to excess for all French fashions, she is only waiting for the end of this little revolution to effect a still greater one in the manners of her country." Such a woman, slightly older than Morris and attending him in the most susceptible state of his young life, was irresistible, and she returned his favor. Responding to a letter in which he expressed a great desire to see her, she wrote, "This wish is in your own Power, but I will say no more on this subject lest I should go too far, as I have once or twice done, only be assured that nothing would give me so much pleasure. . . ."

Not long thereafter, however, Elizabeth convinced Gouverneur to cease his inappropriate pursuit. Although polite letters continued, he never saw her again. He carried a torch for her for a very long time. Arriving in Paris in 1789 he wrote that his heart was "shut up"—and when he learned of her death a year later, he was overcome with grief. "Poor Eliza! My lovely friend; thou art then at Peace and I shall behold thee no more. Never, never, never."

By mid-November 1780, Morris was up and about, but he had withdrawn from consideration for the position in Paris. He returned to his legal work, gaining admission to the bar of the Pennsylvania Supreme Court, and apparently began to improve his finances.

His country's situation was not improving, however. The British military strategy had changed after Saratoga to a concentration on the South. In December 1778, Savannah was captured. When American and French forces could not retake it, the French fleet headed back home. In May 1780, Charleston surrendered to Henry Clinton. Five thousand prisoners and six thousand muskets were lost by the Americans; the British had only seventy-six casualties. It was a bad setback to the American cause, and the summer did not improve matters: "Bloody" Banastre Tarleton beat the Americans at Waxhaws in South Carolina in June, and Cornwallis, who replaced Clinton, outgeneraled Horatio Gates in mid-August, sending Gates on a 180-mile ride to save himself, which effectively destroyed his reputation for good.

Then in October came the pivotal battle of King's Mountain. The ill-advised threats of Major Ferguson, General Cornwallis's man in charge of making a western sweep in the Carolinas, back-fired, for they rallied the "over-mountain" men to come over the Blue Ridge Mountains and attack. They decimated Ferguson and his Tory recruits in an hour, and shifted the Patriot–Tory balance in the area to the Patriot side for the remainder of the war. Cornwallis retreated to South Carolina, and Congress at last accepted Washington's recommendation and replaced Gates with the capable Nathanael Greene, who took charge in December. Greene made a critical decision to split the army, giving half the command to the gifted Daniel Morgan. When Cornwallis sent Tarleton to defeat Morgan, it was Tarleton who lost, and lost badly, at Cowpens, South Carolina. Cornwallis then decided to go after Morgan himself, a decision that gave Greene the opportunity he had hoped for. He headed his troops north at a blistering pace, baiting Cornwallis and stretching the British supply lines too thin. The "Retreat to the Dan River" had the desired effect; Greene reached the river first, crossed it, rested and resupplied his troops, then recrossed it and faced Cornwallis at Guilford Courthouse. Though Cornwallis won the battle, it was a victory too dearly bought—"I never saw such fighting since God made me," Cornwall later wrote. "The Americans fought like demons." He gave up on defeating Greene and returned to Wilmington, North Carolina, leaving a trail of dying wounded.

The stage was now set for the last battles of the war. Cornwallis headed for Virginia, in order to take advantage of its ample resources for supplying his army and to keep the American units from moving south. He arrived in Richmond in mid-June 1781 and started toward Williamsburg. On his arrival, Lafayette, leading a small force, began to harass him. Rochambeau was now the head of French troops in America, and he and Washington had decided on a joint action against the British. French Admiral François Joseph Paul DeGrasse, stationed in Haiti, had advised them that he planned to sail to the Chesapeake with twenty-eight warships and three thousand men and stay until well into the fall.

Henry Clinton had ordered Cornwallis to establish a base for joint operations with the British Navy, and Cornwallis chose Yorktown, on the York River. When Washington heard the French were on their way, he directed Lafayette to keep Cornwallis in Yorktown, and on August 18 Washington and his troops headed south. Though a British naval force had left the Caribbean to follow DeGrasse, they arrived ahead of him, for he had detoured en route to confuse them; he also successfully tricked them into thinking he was heading toward New York. When the British saw no sign of DeGrasse in the Chesapeake, they continued north to New York, joined up with another naval force, and headed south again, still unsure of French intentions.

By the time Washington and the French troops reached Maryland in early September, DeGrasse had provided the promised troops to reinforce Lafayette and blockade the York and James Rivers. On September 5, the naval battle began. DeGrasse had left the bay to prepare to engage the British; it was the French technique of shooting out masts and rigging, rather than the British strategy of firing holes in the enemy's hulls, that quickly won the day for the French, who put six British ships out of action against their loss of four ships. When the British learned that the northern French navy had arrived with a new load of cannon, they realized that they could not help Cornwallis break out of his trap and sailed back to New York.

By the middle of September, Washington, Lafayette, and Rochambeau had agreed on a strategy for the siege of Yorktown, and by the end of the month there were about seventeen thousand American and French troops circling the British, compared to the approximately seven thousand at Cornwallis's disposal. Bombardment began on October 9; ten days later, the British marched out and surrendered.

It was the end of all major military operations. Though the British learned of the rout by the end of November, it would take two more years to get the stubborn king and his Parliament to accept it. Finally, on November 30, 1782, preliminary peace articles were signed, allowing treaty negotiations to begin.

CHAPTER FIVE

THE PUBLIC CREDIT

THREE MONTHS BEFORE YORKTOWN, IN EARLY JULY 1781, Gouverneur Morris had accepted the invitation of Robert Morris—the newly appointed superintendent of finance who was no relation—to become his assistant. Congress, increasingly on the brink of ruin even as victory grew increasingly likely, had decided to appoint executive heads of departments for the war, navy, foreign affairs, and finance. Robert Morris, the financier without whose support the Revolution might well have failed, was given the critical task of heading the last department. The treasury was empty, even though the American economy—despite the war—was in good condition.

Robert Morris, who was eighteen years older than Gouverneur, had come to Philadelphia from England at the age of ten. He was apprenticed to a commercial house as a teenager and later entered into a partnership with the owner's son. The business flourished, and by 1775 it was one of the foremost enterprises in Philadelphia, with investments in merchandise and land. Robert Morris was firmly on the side of independence by the beginning of 1776. A signer of the Declaration of Independence, he was a delegate for Pennsylvania to the Continental Congress from 1775 to 1781, and he almost single-handedly organized the evacuation of Philadelphia before the arrival of the British. He did not hesitate to provide his own funds to the war effort, devoting himself to Congress and its needs. As a source of financial support, Robert was naturally appreciated, but his affable personality also made him well liked in Congress. Even the bilious John Adams described Robert as having "an open Temper and an honest Heart" as well as a "masterly understanding." His extensive mercantile contacts in Europe made him a natural choice for the Committee of Secret Correspondence, whose principal task was establishing a safe mode of communication with countries friendly to the Revolution.

The assignment of the new superintendent and his assistant was, simply, to save the national credit. There were no sources of revenue left to call on. Paper money had depreciated to the point of worthlessness, with the effect of making domestic loans worthless as well.

The first proposal developed by the Morrises and approved by Congress was the establishment of a national bank, which opened on January 7, 1782. The bank was capitalized at $400,000 with $400 shares to be purchased in hard currency ("specie"). The government would accept notes issued by the bank as payment for duties or taxes. Subscriptions to the bank were soon bolstered by the arrival of a large French loan of $254,000 in specie, which Congress permitted to be used to subscribe for shares of the stock on behalf of the national government.

The bank was successful. It helped to reestablish a public sense of security and acted as a tool for postwar commercial ventures by increasing the money supply and encouraging circulation. It was also extremely useful to the government, for it provided advances and permitted negotiation of much more favorable contracts for the military, based on cash payments. The banknotes soon were being accepted at par value throughout the states, thanks to their canny distribution by Robert Morris.

Robert also served as a sort of bank for the benefit of the country by pledging his personal fortune as security for official government notes issued by the Office of Finance. The "Morris notes" were payable on sight and were instantly pressed into service as a reliable means of disbursing public funds. With the useful denominations of twenty, fifty, and eighty dollars, they were a reliable means of exchange in the specie-poor states.

The two men also presented a plan to Congress for confronting and retiring the public debt. Their recommendations accompanied a report prepared in Gouverneur's hand that is still considered a remarkable piece of work. Indeed, it anticipated much of Alexander Hamilton's much more famous *Report on the Public Credit* a decade later. The plan was a logical extension of centralized thinking: the central government would assume all of the war debt, state certificates as well as the continental certificates, and issue percent bonds in exchange. Revenue measures to pay the interest would be straightforward: a land tax ($1 per hundred acres), a poll tax ($1 on all men, free or slave, aged sixteen to sixty), a 5 percent tax on imports, and an excise tax on alcohol. The plan would have encouraged foreign investment in America and helped persuade Americans who had been hoarding money to begin investing; in short, it would have established America's public credit on a firm foundation without the necessity of immediately paying off the principal.

Yet this plan was one in which the *national* good was seen as the goal. For those who identified primarily with their states, the Morrises' recommendations were a threat. These antifederalist leaders demonstrated what Morris described as their "Incompetency of determining what is best for the whole," continuing to behave as "thirteen different Communities whose Rulers are yet ignorant what is best for the single one which they govern." The early years of peacetime would demonstrate the multiple inefficiencies and difficulties of such a situation, but it was in the financial sphere that the shortsightedness would prove nearly fatal. The debt plan fell victim to one of the great bottlenecks created by the Articles of Confederation, the requirement of unanimous ratification. Although Congress approved the amendment, it was clear by the fall of 1782 that Rhode Island would not ratify.

The Morrises knew that the prospect of peace in the air was part of the problem, and that it would take the threat of continued war to force Congress and its constituents to face the need for a stronger central government. Gouverneur had written to Nathanael Greene at the end of 1781:

> Conviction goes but very slowly to the popular Mind but it goes. The Advantages of Union and Decision in carrying on a War. . . . The Waste and Expence and In Efficacy of disjointed Efforts over the Face of an immense Region . . . These must at last induce the People of America (if the war continues) to entrust proper Powers to the American Sovereign as they have already compelled that Sovereign reluctantly to relinquish the Administration & entrust to their Ministers the Care of this immense Republic—I say *if the War continues* for if it does not I have no Hope or Expecta-

tion that the Government will acquire Force *and I will go farther I have no Hope that our Union can subsist except in the Form of an absolute monarchy* and this does not seem to consist with *the Taste and Temper of the People.*

Peace was definitely on the way, and a year after the letter the situation was worse than ever.

It was at this dire juncture, when everything seemed on the verge of falling apart, that Gouverneur turned to the army. They were the largest and angriest group of creditors, and he believed that they could alarm Congress sufficiently to take the steps he and Robert Morris believed were absolutely critical to the new nation's survival. In his passionate pursuit of this goal, Gouverneur came close to what many considered the encouragement of treason among the troops. Yet for men such as the Morrises, the stakes in this battle with Congress were as high as any that had taken place in the field. Despite the victory at Yorktown, the winding down of the war did not mean that the underlying difficulties of the war effort had been solved. When one considers how heart-stoppingly close to disaster America seemed to be after winning a war against one of the greatest powers in the world, the desperation of the Morrises is understandable.

The Newburgh Conspiracy took place in the winter of 1783. The army knew that the fighting was nearly over, but when they looked to their own futures, matters were bleak, for they saw a Congress that was near bankruptcy with no apparent means of paying any of its obligations, including those to the army. Most of the officers had had to rely on their own assets to survive, and many were heavily in debt. For the enlisted men matters were worse: a year's wages or more were overdue. Years of war had made the men cynical, and they knew it was entirely possible that Congress and their country would attempt to avoid their obligations to the army altogether. They justifiably felt ill-used and angry. Many of the enlisted men were very young, which made the potential for volatility even greater.

In early January 1783, three of Washington's officers came to Philadelphia from their winter camp at Newburgh on the Hudson, New York, with a petition to Congress. Washington wrote to Congress, "The patience and long-sufferance of this army are almost exhausted," and the petition was made with his tacit consent. The Morrises, Alexander Hamilton, and the other nationalists saw this as their chance to pressure Congress to adopt national revenue measures. Gouverneur wrote an extraordinary letter to John Jay:

> The Army have Swords in their hands. . . . I am glad to see Things in their present Train. Depend on it good will arise from the Situation to which we are hastening. And this you may rely on that my Efforts will not be wanting. I pledge to you on the present occasion, and while I think it probable that much Convulsion will ensue Yet it must terminate in giving to the Government that power without which Government is but a Name. Government in America is not possessed of it but the People are well prepared. Wearied with War, their Acquiescence may be depended on with absolute Certainty and you and I my friend know by experience that when a few Men of Sense and Spirit get together and declare that they are the Authority such few as are of a different Opinion may easily be convinced of their Mistake by that powerful Argument the Halter.

Robert Morris told Congress that unless provisions for funding the debt were made, he would resign. Congress was shaken by the threat, and by the officers' hints about the army's discontent. It directed Robert to issue a month's pay to the officers and soldiers in February, but it rejected a proposal to award a "commutation pay" bonus. The Morrises decided to encourage the army to make stronger—perhaps more menacing—gestures. Gouverneur wrote to Henry Knox and Nathanael Greene to ask for their support, but he was turned down flat. Hamilton also wrote to Washington, telling him to put aside his customary "delicacy" and take action.

Whether incited by the encouragement of the nationalists or the internal forces of discontent, a clique centered on the ever-disgruntled Horatio Gates was gathering. An incendiary petition circulated throughout the camp expressing the army's outrage at Congress's tepid response, blaming the earlier petition's "milk-and-water style," and calling on the troops to refuse to disperse if peace should shortly be declared. If the war continued, the troops were to go as a body to the frontier, leaving the country defenseless.

Some historians view the petition (known as the "Newburgh Address") and the events surrounding it as proof of an intent to mutiny. Others see it as rhetoric intended to galvanize Congress. However, few historians have believed that nationalists like Hamilton and the Morrises ever intended an actual coup and the installation of another government. In any event, no coup took place. Washington, to the surprise of the agitators, moved quickly to issue a condemnation of the address and called his own meeting on March 15, setting the stage for a famous scene in which the wily statesman first fumbled for his glasses so that he could read a letter to his assembled officers and then told them, "I have already grown gray in the service of my country. I am now going blind." It was a master stroke and brought the assemblage to tears. They unanimously endorsed resolutions condemning the address and affirming their confidence in Congress and Washington.

Washington's denunciation of the address was the end of the affair. But Washington apparently thought that the officers were involved in more than a game of brinkmanship with Congress and that Gouverneur Morris had written the address. As such, it was the one time that Washington was driven to believe the worst of Morris, describing him as an "insidious foe" who was plotting the ruin of the military and civilian government by "sowing the seeds of discord and separation between them." It was not until a second address was circulated immediately after Washington's confrontation with his men that the general realized it would have been impossible for Morris to have written either of them. In fact, the author was Major John Armstrong, a vitriolic young man and a close associate of Gates.

The incident at Newburgh alarmed Congress, as the Morrises and Hamilton had hoped. Congress voted to give officers five years of full pay and enlisted men four months' pay, though it sidestepped immediate payment with furloughs. It was not quite the end of the army's discontent, however. In June 1783, some three hundred furloughed soldiers marched on Congress in Philadelphia and demanded payment, threatening to hold the delegates as hostages. When word came that the military was en route to arrest them, they promptly surrendered, but it was enough to send Congress scrambling to Princeton, New Jersey, and eventually to New York for the next several years.

On April 11, 1783, before being chased out of Philadelphia, Congress received the treaty with Britain and directed the end of hostilities.

CHAPTER SIX

THE CONSTITUTION

THE END OF THE WAR MEANT THAT MORRIS COULD AT LAST return to Morrisania to see his mother, Sarah. For Sarah, now in her late sixties, the war had been a terrible ordeal. Her claim for the British ravages to Morrisania's timber and livestock came to eight thousand pounds, but her stepson Staats, in whose name the claim was pursued in England, would get only about one-sixth of that amount. She would survive less than three more years. In the final year of her life, Richard Morris, another of Gouverneur's half-brothers, would sue her for an accounting of the estate, alleging malfeasance. When she died, he substituted Gouverneur and Staats as defendants.

For the moment, Morris decided to continue living in Philadelphia. Before long, he and Robert Morris left the finance office and began doing business together, putting money into trade with China and Europe and speculating in American lands. The parcels were vast. Gouverneur bought tracts of eight thousand and two thousand acres in Pennsylvania, and in 1787 a group the Morrises belonged to bought a huge parcel along the St. Lawrence River in New York. Gouverneur's stake was about sixty thousand acres, paid for with a bond that named Robert as surety. Gouverneur also invested in the inventor John Fitch's project to develop a steamboat.

In 1787, Gouverneur acquired the family estate of Morrisania when his half-brother Staats, who had taken possession on the death of Sarah, decided to sell it. Gouverneur got along well with the affable but gout-ridden Staats, but the transaction was slowed by Richard's lawsuit. The purchase price consisted of a waiver of Gouverneur's patrimonial share due from Staats, a mortgage to Richard and to Staats, and agreement by his sisters to defer collection on their share of the patrimony, which would now come to them through Gouverneur. The net obligation for Gouverneur was about 7,500 pounds, a sizeable amount for that time.

The commercial atmosphere of the postwar years was intoxicating for those who could take advantage of the opportunities, but it was also a period in which the defects of the weak Articles of Confederation became crippling. Americans were increasingly frustrated by the impotence of the central government against the encroachment of the states upon what was perceived as the federal sphere and its inability to impose taxes and other revenue measures that would keep the United States creditworthy. Other issues included establishing a uniform currency, the need to have the federal government hold and control the western lands, and ineffective organization at the federal level. The discontent also arose from the defects in the state governments themselves. Morris had identified such problems with the New York state constitution, writing to Hamilton in 1777:

That there are Faults in it is not to be wondered at for it is the Work of Men and of Men perhaps not the best qualified for such Undertakings. I think it deficient for the Want of Vigor in the executive unstable from the very Nature of popular elective Governments and dilatory from the Complexity of the Legislature.

In 1786, several states agreed to send delegates to Annapolis, Maryland, to discuss commercial issues. Although only five states attended, they recommended that a second convention be convened in Philadelphia in May 1787 in order to "render the Constitution of the Federal Government adequate to the exigencies of the Union."

Morris was chosen as one of the seven delegates sent by Pennsylvania to the Constitutional Convention. His election was no sure thing; one Philadelphian wrote to his brother on January 5, 1787, that "Bobby [Robert Morris] [had] sufficient influence to carry Gouverneur [as a delegate] however improper it was to choose an alien for he is certainly a Yorker, besides the trouble he will give by his vanity & schemes." Morris must have anticipated opposition of this sort. He had, he wrote to Knox, "declared in general my unwillingness to accept of any Thing under this State," but he was out of town when the vote took place. "Had the Object been any other than it is, I would have declined," Morris told Knox, but the purpose of the Convention was too important and Morris accepted his fate.

It was a lucky thing for his country. Morris would prove one of the most powerful speakers at the Convention. Some historians judge that he had more influence on the Constitution than anyone other than James Madison and James Wilson. His coruscating facility with language kept him on his feet—he spoke 173 times, more than any other delegate—constantly suggesting, debating,

Fig. 5: Independence Hall, the site of the Constitutional Convention of 1787, where Morris gave some of the most eloquent speeches that were heard that summer and wrote the Constitution's final draft.

challenging, and, when it came to the written results, burnishing the document that was wrung out of the fifty-five delegates who came to Philadelphia during that miserably hot summer. He impressed most, but not all, of his fellow delegates. One complained that Morris "throws around him such a glare that he charms, captivates, and leads away the senses of all who hear him. With an infinite stretch of fancy he brings to view things when he is engaged in deep argumentation, that render all the labor of reasoning easy and pleasing. But with all these powers he is fickle and inconstant,—never pursuing one train of thinking—nor ever regular."

One recent historian, Jack Rakove has similarly dismissed Morris, saying that "for lawyerly solipsism, Morris had few peers," but that is a gross undervaluation of his contribution.* The delegates often turned down his proposals (though it is worth noting that Madison, the generally acknowledged "Father of the Constitution," was on the "losing" side of forty of the seventy-one proposals he advocated), but his energetic participation meant that the debates were as full in the round as time and mental energy permitted, and there is no doubt that the Constitution was a far better-designed piece of work than it would have been without Morris. Moreover, though he might take sides for the sake of deepening the debate of each element, his fundamental convictions and ideas on how best to achieve them were consistent and had been so since the days of drafting the New York constitution. Morris's influence was most strongly felt in the design of the Senate as a legislative branch equal in power to the House of Representatives, in the creation of a strong executive, and in the related issues of westward expansion and slavery.

Throughout the Convention, Morris promoted a balanced governmental structure with three functions: moderating the influence of the popular will, keeping the executive independent of the legislature, and ensuring the commitment of the rich to the scheme. This would secure civil liberty (the right to have property, and the right to be left alone) and political liberty (the right to hold government answerable to the people and the right to participate in the government through voting). Civil liberty, in Morris's view, was the most important, because without it political liberty could not survive. He therefore supported property requirements for the members of both houses, agreeing with Madison that this

---

* Actually, it is not clear what Mr. Rakove meant here by "solipsism," but the comment and the context make it obvious that he does not consider Morris an important part of the Convention.

was the only way to protect property-holders from an electorate composed of people without property; as Madison put it, there was "no reason why the rights of property which chiefly bears the burden of Government and is so much an object of Legislation should not be respected as well as personal rights in the choice of Rulers." Morris put it differently: property, he said, is "the main object of Society."

On May 25, the Convention opened in the Pennsylvania State House, and Washington was unanimously elected president of the Convention. He was ushered up the aisle by Edmund Randolph and took his place in the magnificent mahogany "rising sun" chair in front, where he would maintain a dignified silence for the majority of the summer. Delegates would come and go; Morris himself disappeared for the month of June, attending to previous commitments at Morrisania.

The first step was to decide the rules under which the Convention would be conducted. It was agreed that seven states would form a quorum (Rhode Island and New Hampshire were not present). Before the Convention had begun, Morris had argued for rules that would give the smaller states less clout; the delegates quickly agreed that no state would have a veto, and votes would be determined by a majority of the states actually present at the time. Proceedings were to be kept secret, a decision that Jefferson later denounced but was essential. With concurrent public scrutiny, Madison later said, the Constitution could never have been drafted.

The first substantive work took place when Edmund Randolph presented James Madison's "Virginia Plan," a set of fifteen resolutions that encapsulated the conclusions Madison had drawn in his study of constitutional design and government in the months leading up to the Convention. The first resolution was a proposal to correct and enlarge the Articles of Confederation; the remainder contained the specific suggestions for doing so. The Madisonian design included a bicameral legislature (with one branch popularly elected and the second branch named by the first), federal judges, and an executive magistrate.

Alexander Hamilton took the floor and argued that the delegates must first decide whether there would be a single national government or a confederation of states bound together by treaty. The next day, Randolph, using material prepared by Morris, proposed an alternative initial resolution in three parts, the third of which, a resolution that "a *national* Government ought to be established consisting of a *supreme* Legislature, Executive [and] Judiciary," was passed, after some debate about the word "supreme." Morris stated flatly that the word was essential to establish the national power; "a federal agreement which each party may violate at pleasure cannot answer the purpose. . . . [W]e had better take a supreme government now than a despot twenty years hence—for come he must."

The delegates then turned to the specifics of the Virginia Plan and began to discuss the extremely difficult question of allotting representation in the two branches; at this point Morris left Philadelphia for the month of June. When he returned to the floor of the Convention on July 2, the matter was still unresolved but had evolved to a tie vote on giving each state equal representation in the Senate. Morris, like Madison, opposed equal state representation in either house; moreover, he believed that *state* representation was not the proper role of the Senate. The issue implicated Morris's strong convictions regarding the need for a government to contain checks and balances to harness the inevitable abusive tendencies of both the populace and the wealthy. Madison would describe this view as Morris's incessant focus on "the political depravity of men, and the necessity of checking one vice and interest by opposing to them another vice [and] interest." Madison's own constitutional creeds were similar. Morris's skepticism about human nature and its effect on government has been vindicated time and again in the history of the United States, yet it did not mean that he despaired of a successful constitution: rather, his pragmatic insistence on that skepticism as a guiding rule was for him the essential tool that would allow imperfect humans to achieve a workable and efficient republic with the greatest good to the many. He also was determined to push for a national sense of identity that would overcome and dissolve localism and the parochialism of the individual states' interests. In his view, the proposed Senate failed on both counts.

Morris therefore opposed what would come to be described as the "Great Compromise" (really a victory for the less populous states rather than a compromise) that structured the Senate with equal representation from the states. Morris instead sought appointment of senators by the executive without regard to residence. In Morris's view, the smaller states' claim of a right to be protected from the hegemony of the larger states was baseless: although the Articles of Confederation had provided them an equal vote, this had been, as he put it flatly, "extorted" from the larger states in a time of crisis and should have no influence in the current deliberations: "Standing now on that ground, they [the smaller states] demand under the new system greater rights as men, than their fellow Citizens of the large States. The proper answer to them is that the same necessity of which they formerly took advantage, does not now exist, and that the large states are at liberty now to consider what is right, rather than what may be expedient." This structuring of the Senate, in his opinion, badly interfered with the goal of exterminating state allegiances and localism, as well as the need for a national consciousness. Like Madison, Morris's experiences had left him with little respect for the governments of the states or their abilities to rise above local prejudices and interests for the good of the entire country. "[W]hat if all the Charters [and] Constitutions of the States were thrown into the fire and all their demagogues into the ocean. What would it be to the happiness of America?" he asked, probably only partly in jest. "State attachments, and State importance have been the bane of this Country. We can not annihilate; but we may perhaps take out the teeth of the serpents."

To support his claim, Morris pointed to Europe:

> The same circumstances which unite the people here, unite them in Germany. They have there a common language, a common law, common usages and manners, and a common interest in being united; yet their local jurisdictions destroy every tie. . . . The United Netherlands are at this time torn in factions. With these examples before our eyes shall we form establishments which must necessarily produce the same effects. It is of no consequence from what districts the [second] branch shall be drawn, if it be so constituted as to yield an asylum ag[ainst] these evils.

However, in Morris's view there was more at stake than the problem of small states' improper share of power. His concept of the Senate's function was quite different from those who saw the Senate as a means of balancing the power of the most populous states in the House with a branch in which the states were equally powerful. The balance he perceived as essential was of the inevitable American aristocracy—the wealthy—against the "democratic"†

---

† "Democracy" as used in the political debate of the time referred to popular election of a legislature or a body with all governmental functions; though we

tendencies represented by the House. He reminded the delegates of their own experiences with their states' "democratic branches" (the popularly elected lower houses of state legislatures), which had demonstrated precipitateness, changeableness, and "excesses against personal liberty, private property, and personal safety."

At the same time, he urged, the wealthy had to be checked. He had long recognized the frailties of the rich and believed that their tendency to abuse their power could be curbed only if they were invested in the government. He told his well-to-do fellow delegates candidly: "The Rich will strive to establish their dominion [and] enslave the rest. They always did. They always will. The proper security ag[ainst] them is to form them into a separate interest. The two forces will then control each other. Let the rich mix with the poor and in a Commercial country they will establish an oligarchy. Take away commerce and the democracy will triumph." It was a theme he would sound repeatedly throughout the Convention. Without hesitation, Morris told his affluent colleagues that he "fear[ed] the influence of the rich: They will have the same effect here as elsewhere if we do not . . . keep them within their proper sphere. We should remember that the people never act from reason alone. The Rich will take advantage of their passions [and] make these the instruments for oppressing them. The Result of the Contest will be a violent aristocracy or a more violent despotism." The solution was to separate the rich into their own branch: the Senate. "By thus combining [and] setting apart the aristocratic interest, the popular interest will be combined [against] it. There will be a mutual check and mutual security."

---

tend to call America a "democracy" today it is in fact a republic as the Founding Fathers understood it. "Democracy" was considered as tantamount to mob rule.

Morris's aim was not simply to check the vices of each side but also to put the abilities of the self-made men of the Senate at the service of their country. In this connection, Morris was quite open in his view that "great personal property" should be a requirement for the senators, for it demonstrated "private industry, which is a signification of their private virtue." By the same token, Morris opposed the move to exclude senators from holding judicial or executive positions in the government: "[S]hall the best, the most able, the most virtuous citizens not be permitted to hold offices? Who then are to hold them?" he asked. Despite the fact that many delegates agreed with Morris on this issue, including Madison, it was Morris who was accused of being an aristocrat. The same accusation would be made in France, and his response, as recorded by Madison, was sharp:

> He had long learned not to be the dupe of words. The sound of Aristocracy therefore had no effect on him. It was the thing, not the name, to which he was opposed, and one of his principal objections to the Constitution as it is now before us, is that it threatens this Country with an Aristocracy. The aristocracy will grow out of the House of Representatives. Give the votes to people who have no property, and they will sell them to the rich who will be able to buy them.

The delegates did not adopt Morris's recommendation for the Senate. However, he was successful, along with Rufus King, in retaining one small but powerful structural change that would allow legislators to promote national rather than local interests: the provision that the senators could vote as individuals instead of by state.

The design of the national executive branch was one of the most difficult tasks undertaken by the Convention, for in this there was no real experience in the state governments: they were charting unknown territory. As Morris noted, "It is the most difficult of all rightly to balance the Executive. Make him too weak: The Legislature will usurp his powers. Make him too strong: He will usurp on the legislature." All agreed that the Continental Congress had failed largely because it lacked any executive at all, much less a vigorous one. This had been due to an understandable aversion to anything reminiscent of monarchy, yet they had found that a legislature could not legislate and execute at the same time. The "cabinet" created in 1781 with Robert Morris and others had attempted to address this issue but had still been frustrated by the limited power of the Continental Congress.

Gouverneur's national and state experiences made him a fervent advocate of a vigorous executive, but when he was accused of thereby advocating a monarchy he retorted that he was "as little a friend to monarchy as any gentleman. . . . The way to keep out monarchichal Gov[ernment] was to establish such a Repub[lican] gov[overnment] as would make the people happy and prevent a desire of change."

One "great object" of an executive, argued Morris, was to "control the Legislature. The Legislature will continually seek to aggrandize [and] perpetuate themselves; and will seize those critical moments produced by war, invasion or convulsion for that purpose." The executive must be "the guardian of the people, even of the lower classes, [against] Legislative tyranny, against the Great [and] the wealthy who in the course of things will necessarily compose the Legislative body."

Simply creating two branches of the legislature to balance each other would *not* act to check the overall potential for legislative abuse of power, or what Morris called "legislative tyranny." "On the contrary," he said, "it may favor it, and if the first branch can be seduced may find the means of success. The Executive therefore ought to be so constituted as to be the great protector of the Mass of the people."

In order to perform this protective function, the executive had to be a "national" official, elected directly by the people, not appointed by the Legislature, as many delegates advocated. Morris was adamant on this point. On July 17, he told them: "If the Legislature elect, it will be the work of intrigue, of cabal, and of faction; it will be like the election of a pope by a conclave of cardinals; real merit will rarely be the title to the appointment. "A week later, he reiterated, "Of all possible modes of appointment that by the Legislature is the worst." "If the Legislature is to appoint, and to impeach or to influence the impeachment, the Executive will be the mere creature of it. . . . The Legislature is worthy of unbounded confidence in some respects, and liable to equal distrust in others."

It is noteworthy that Morris, so often labeled an elitist, believed that the American people, voting directly, would make the best choice: "If the people should elect, they will never fail to prefer some man of distinguished character, or services; some man, if [I] might so speak, of continental reputation."

Morris also argued that the president should be eligible for reelection, contrary to the views of many who believed this opened the door to monarchy. Rather, he said, prohibiting reelection would tend "to destroy the great motive to good behavior, the hope of being *rewarded* by a re-appointment. It was saying to [the executive] make hay while the sun shines." Moreover, Morris suggested, taking away the hope of reappointment "may give a dangerous turn to one of the strongest passions in the human breast. The love of fame is the great spring to noble and illustrious actions. Shut the Civil road to Glory and he may be compelled to seek it by the sword. . . ." Benjamin Franklin disagreed, remarking sanctimoniously that "[i]n free governments the rulers are the servants, and the people their superiors. . . . For the former therefore to return among the latter was not to *degrade* but to *promote* them." Morris responded promptly that "he had no doubt our executive" would be modest enough "to decline the promotion."

Despite these strong arguments by Morris, on July 26 George Mason successfully moved to endorse the original concept of a seven-year term without eligibility for reelection, and appointment of the president by the national legislature. But the battle was not over yet: Morris's chance came when he was named to the "Committee of Eleven" to work on "unfinished parts." When the committee reported on September 4, the delegates were surprised to find that the seven-year single term had been replaced with a four-year term and re-eligibility. Moreover, the committee had replaced appointment by the national legislature with what was essentially the Electoral College system. Morris took the floor to defend the provisions. What they proposed was not direct popular election; but it was much closer to the electorate than the idea of appointment by the legislature, and Morris hoped it would ensure the executive's independence of the legislature and of the individual states. After the delegates made changes to provide for runoff elections to be conducted by the House, the provision was approved.

The Committee of Eleven had also inserted a vice president, a concept that hadn't previously been approved, who would be the runner-up in electoral votes and next in line to the presidency, and who would act as president of the Senate. One of the delegates complained about the Senate position, arguing that the "close intimacy which must subsist between the president and vice president makes it absolutely improper." Morris, always quick on his feet, replied that "the vice president then will be the first heir apparent that ever loved his father."

Morris also argued that the executive should have an absolute veto: "The most virtuous Citizens will often as members of a legislative body concur in measures which afterwards in their private capacity they will be ashamed of. Encroachments of the popular branch of the Government ought to be guarded against. . . . If the Executive be overturned by the popular branch, as happened in England, the tyranny of one man will ensue." In the face of a refusal to adopt the absolute veto, he proposed a veto with a three-quarters override requirement, but that too failed; the Convention voted 6–4 to adopt the two-thirds override rule.

The question of slavery was closely bound together with the issue of future admission of new states from the western territories and the proper rule of representation in the House, although the fear that southwestern expansion would mean the spread of slavery was not debated directly. (Interestingly, the Constitution avoids the word "slavery" altogether, reflecting the fact that no matter how much they might defend the institution, none of the delegates believed it was a word that belonged in the constitution of a republican government.) At least one scholar who has examined Morris's work at the Convention has concluded that Morris's efforts to use the Constitution to keep the balance of power in the "Atlantic" states as the country expanded westward was based on his unstated but unvarying goal of keeping slavery from spreading westward. It was not until he failed in this effort, however, that he felt free to excoriate slavery in perhaps the most eloquent speech heard that summer in the Convention.

At first, however, he attempted to achieve this result by other routes. On July 9 he delivered the report of a committee appointed to consider the issue, which recommended that the Constitution simply declare the initial number of representatives for the new government based on one representative per forty thousand inhabitants and leave the allocation of representation, based on wealth and population, open for the national legislature to determine based on future circumstances and the "relative importance" of new states. The number of representatives allocated to northern and southern states brought complaints from the southern members, who argued that if "the regulation of trade is to be given to the General Government," the southern states "will be nothing more than overseers for the Northern States," and said that in view of their "superior wealth" the southerners expected equality, not minority status. They feared, moreover, that the North would act to keep its majority even if wealth and population grew to be dominant in the South and West. Morris rose and told the delegates that he "regretted the turn of the debate. The States, he found, had many representatives on the floor. Few, he feared, were to be deemed the Representatives of America. He thought the Southern States have, by the Report, more than their share of representation."

The debate over the way in which wealth and numbers should be used went in circles. The Convention then considered Edmund Randolph's motion for requiring the government to conduct a periodic census, including three-fifths of the slave population, and to make an estimation of wealth and adjust the representation on that basis. Morris saw that this might well result in a "preponderancy into the Western Scale" because "in time the Western people [would] outnumber the Atlantic States," and he suggested that the Convention insert "the power of the latter to keep a majority of votes in their own hands." This was not republican language, but it did make sense, for the western states might very well have interests that would conflict badly with those of the Atlantic states—as Morris suggested a few days later, they "will inevitably bring on a war with Spain for the Mississippi," even though, "having no property nor interest exposed on the sea," they would be "little affected by such a war." The other interest that would conflict with those of the northern states was, of course, slavery.

The principal argument made by the advocates of slavery, who sought to protect the institution by increasing their power in the federal government, was that population was a measure of wealth; wealth, which included slaves, would determine taxation; and therefore the votes should be allotted on that basis. Morris objected that "the number of inhabitants was not a proper standard of wealth" and asked why, if slaves were considered as wealth, was "no other wealth but slaves included"? He again argued that the existing states should be able to keep the dominant power if other states were later admitted, suggesting that the residents of the new and raw western territories would not provide representatives with the same political expertise as the older eastern states.

Some members from the South saw this for what it probably was: an effort to hold the power to stop the spread of slavery. William Davie of North Carolina announced that it was "high time now to speak out." He "saw that it was meant by some gentlemen to deprive the Southern States of any share of representation for their blacks. He was sure that North Carolina would never confederate on any terms that did not rate them at least as three-fifths. If the Eastern States meant, therefore, to exclude them altogether, the business was at an end." Madison recorded Morris's answer to Davie:

It has been said that it is high time to speak out. As one member, he would candidly do so. He came here to form a compact for the good of America. He was ready to do so with all the States. He hoped, and believed, that all would enter into such a compact. If they would not, he was ready to join with any States that would. But as the compact was to be voluntary, it is in vain for the Eastern States to insist on what the Southern States will never agree to. It is equally vain for the latter to require, what the other States can never admit; and he verily believed the people of Pennsylvania will never agree to a representation of negroes. What can be desired by these States more than has been already proposed—that the Legislature shall from time to time regulate representation according to population and wealth.

In Morris's view, the division between large and small states on the unresolved matter of representation in the Senate had become a division between northern and southern states in the debate over apportioning representation in the House. Was that division a genuine one? he asked. "[I]f fictitious let it be dismissed [and] let us proceed with due confidence. If it be real, instead of attempting to blend incompatible things, let us at once take a friendly leave of each other. There can be no end of demands for security if every particular interest is to be entitled to it. The Eastern States may claim it for their fishery, and for other objects, as the South[ern] States claim it for their peculiar objects."

Pierce Butler of South Carolina replied: "The security the South[ern] States want is that their negroes may not be taken from them, which some gentlemen within or without doors, have a very good mind to do."

Unfortunately for Morris, the arguments he had to make to oppose giving the South and West the power to perpetuate slavery were not consistent with his own positions regarding the right of representation. James Wilson, no friend to slavery, nonetheless appears to have ignored the shadow debate that was taking place when he rose and declaimed against Morris's position: "If the interior Country should acquire [a] majority, it will not only have the right [to govern the minority] but will avail themselves of it whether we will or no. . . . Further, if numbers be not a proper rule, why is not some better rule pointed out."

The motion on the census passed. However, Morris had one more chance; when the census language was presented to the Convention by the Committee of Detail on August 8, Morris moved to have the word "free" inserted in front of "inhabitants." He had traveled in Virginia in early 1785 and his comments reflected his observations:

> He never would concur in upholding domestic slavery. It was a nefarious institution. It was the curse of heaven on the States where it prevailed. Compare the free regions of the Middle States, where a rich [and] noble cultivation marks the prosperity [and] happiness of the people, with the misery [and] poverty which overspread the barren wastes of Va. Mary[land] [and] the other States having slaves. Travel thro' the whole Continent [and] you behold the prospect continually varying with the appearance [and] disappearance of slavery. The moment you leave the E. Sts. [and] enter New York, the effects of the institution become visible, passing thro' the Jerseys [and] entering Pa. every criterion of superior improvement witnesses the change. Proceed south[wardly] [and] every step you take thro' the great region of slaves presents a desert increasing, with the increasing proportion of these wretched beings.

Morris then began one of the greatest speeches of his career. "Upon what principle is it," he asked, while Madison's fingers flew to take down every biting word,

that the slaves shall be computed in the representation? Are they men? Then make them Citizens and let them vote. Are they property? Why then is no other property included? The Houses in this city [Philadelphia] are worth more than all the wretched slaves which cover the rice swamps of South Carolina. The admission of slaves into the Representation when fairly explained comes to this: that the inhabitant of Georgia and S.C. who goes to the Coast of Africa, and in defiance of the most sacred laws of humanity tears away his fellow creatures from their dearest connections [and] damns them to the most cruel bondages, shall have more votes in a Govt. instituted for protection of the rights of mankind, than the Citizen of Pa. or N. Jersey who views with a laudable horror, so nefarious a practice.

Domestic slavery is the most prominent feature in the aristocratic countenance of the proposed Constitution. The vassalage of the poor has ever been the favorite offspring of Aristocracy. And What is the proposed compensation to the Northern States for a sacrifice of every principle of right, of every impulse of humanity. They are to bind themselves to march their militia for the defence of the S. States; for their defence agst. those very slaves of whom they complain. They must supply vessels [and] seamen in case of foreign Attack. The Legislature will have indefinite power to tax them by excises, and duties on imports: both of which will fall heavier on them than on the Southern inhabitants; for the bohea tea used by a Northern freeman, will pay more tax than the whole consumption of the miserable slave, which consists of nothing more than his physical subsistence and the rag that covers his nakedness. On the other side the Southern States are not to be restrained from importing fresh supplies of wretched Africans, at once to increase the danger of attack, and the difficulty of defence; nay they are to be encouraged to it by an assurance of having their votes in the Natl. Govt. increased in proportion, and are at the same time to have their exports [and] their slaves exempt from all contributions for the public service. Let it not be said that direct taxation is to be proportioned to representation. It is idle to suppose that the Genl. Govt. can stretch its hand directly into the pockets of the people scattered over so vast a Country. They can only do it through the medium of exports imports [and] excises. For what then are all these sacrifices to be made? He would sooner submit himself to a tax for paying for all the negroes in the U. States, than saddle posterity with such a Constitution.

There can be no doubt that this splendid speech, unsurpassed for eloquence and passion by any other in the Convention, made him enemies in the southern states. The South Carolinians decided to be equally blunt. "If slavery be wrong," declared Charles Pinckney, "it is justified by the example of all the world."

In the end, of course, as Morris had feared, the smaller states chose to protect their own particular interests through the Senate and agreed to the three-fifths rule for the House and to a fugitive slave law.

It is a measure of the respect Morris had earned that his fellow delegates chose him, grudgingly or not, to draft the separate articles into the final document. According to Madison, "The *finish* given to the style and arrangement of the Constitution fairly belongs to the pen of Mr. Morris; the task having, probably, been handed over to him by the chairman of the Committee of Style, himself a highly respected member, and with the ready concurrence of the others. A better choice could not have been made, as the performance of the task proved."

On September 17, 1787, the weary delegates came together for the last time, and most, but not all, signed the document. On the 18th, Washington ate with Robert Morris and Gouverneur Morris at Robert's house, and the three rode out together to the floating bridge at Gray's Ferry, where they parted. Washington headed toward Mt. Vernon; Gouverneur returned to Morrisania and to business, refusing Hamilton's request to push for ratification by contributing to the *Federalist*. Robert's business affairs were not in good order, and Gouverneur needed to make money to pay for Morrisania.

A quarter of a century later, Morris would write about the making of the Constitution. During the Convention, he said, "My faculties were on the stretch to further our business, remove impediments, obviate objections, and conciliate jarring opinions." Then, in a burst of disappointed but realistic bitterness born of years of clear-eyed observation, he wrote:

> But, after all, what does it signify, that men should have a written Constitution, containing unequivocal provisions and limitations? The legislative lion will not be entangled in the meshes of a logical net. The legislature will always make the power which it wishes to exercise, unless it be so organized as to contain within itself the sufficient check. Attempts to restrain it from outrage by other means will only render it more outrageous. The idea of binding legislators by oaths is puerile.

The two hundred years of American history that have followed since Morris wrote these bleak words have provided repeated examples of their truth; but the same history has demonstrated the lasting genius and power of the document Morris helped create.

Fig. 6: The U.S. Constitution, with Morris's powerful words of introduction: "We the People of the United States." By using these words instead of a list of the thirteen states, Morris's masterful editing forced the document to transcend state identities and speak for all Americans.

CHAPTER SEVEN

FRANCE

———

IN DECEMBER 1788, ONE YEAR AND THREE MONTHS AFTER signing the Constitution, Gouverneur Morris, now thirty-six years old, went to the New York pier and boarded the *Henrietta* for Europe. His mission was business: primarily the mending of Robert's affairs, which had begun to falter and would in fact never recover.

Robert had many ventures, including a partnership he had formed in 1784 with Gouverneur and William Constable, a wily Philadelphia businessman who (perhaps unbeknownst to the Morrises) had served both sides as a merchant during the Revolutionary War. Gouverneur's share of Constable, Rucker & Co., was five thousand pounds New York currency, which he would pay back to Robert from the profits or in exchange for his legal services. The firm was one of the first to engage in trade with the Chinese, which would prove profitable, and it also traded with Europe. In July 1787, however, the firm's principals had suffered an unexpected setback when they learned that one of their agents in Europe had defaulted on a number of Robert's bills. The news spread rapidly in Philadelphia, and Gouverneur was dispatched to Europe to try to rectify the situation.

He was also directed to salvage Robert's tobacco contract with a quasi-governmental entity called the French Farmers General. The contract had been considered an enormously profitable coup when it was negotiated in late 1784, but it was in trouble. This was partly due to late shipments but even more to the efforts of the current minister to France, Thomas Jefferson, who had gone to Paris with the specific intention of scuttling the contract. Gouverneur was supposed to save the agreement, to seek other contracts for goods such as flour, to sell American lands, and, if possible, to purchase the American war debt to France at a discount.

Morris landed at Havre at the end of January 1789 and proceeded to Paris with his manservant, taking up rooms near the Palais Royale. Within two weeks, probably as an antidote to loneliness, he purchased several blank journals and began keeping a diary. Exhibiting his usual self-discipline, he would keep it until nearly the last day of his life, with only one long interlude of silence—the period of the Terror. Unlike Jefferson, who near the end of his life wrote his own remembrances and edited them with careful hindsight the better to embellish a legend of far-seeing wisdom, these volumes are what the law of evidence calls "present-sense impression." They contain such powerful imprints of Morris's effervescent personality, his curiosity about people and enjoyment of their company, his observations on America and Europe and politics and love and power and cruelty and misery, that it is difficult to believe that he wrote them more than two hundred years ago. They are a national treasure.

Upon his arrival in Paris, Morris immediately began to make the social rounds, carrying letters of introduction from Washington, Franklin, and others. French society at the end of the ancien régime was nothing like American society, and though he was scarcely naïve, Morris was shocked by what he saw. Extramarital relations were commonplace. Faithful married couples were the subject of derision, while marriages "of the heart" (not to one's spouse) were admired. At a dinner party not long after his arrival, Morris recorded a "Striking Instance" of what he delicately termed "the Facility of Manners" demonstrated by the Vicomte de Ségur, a well-known Lothario. After dinner, Ségur asked a woman at the dinner to

> show him Something in her Cabinet [her room] and goes directly towards it. She in a Minute expresses Anxiety lest he should see her Papers and follows him, leaving us in the Salon. . . . He opens the Door and in the Quotation from a Play announces the Intention. Shuts and bolts it. After a convenient Time Madame cries: "Monsr. Morris! Monsr. Morris!" . . . Her son, finding the Door bolted, runs round thro another Way. She comes in asking if I did not hear her cry Au Secours!—I answer "Oui Madame," with great Sangfroid. . . . [H]aving thus, as Sterne says, gratified the Sentiment, in a few Minutes [Ségur] takes Leave. . . .

Blatant promiscuity was not the only vice that alienated Morris. A few months after his arrival, hearing that an innocent baker had been beheaded, Morris wrote in his diary that Paris was "perhaps as wicked a Spot as exists. Incest, Murder, Bestiality, Fraud, Rapine, Oppression, Baseness, Cruelty; and yet this is the City which has stepped forward in the sacred Cause of Liberty." These impressions were tempered by his introduction to Guillaume-Chrétien de

Lamoignon de Malesherbes, the retired statesman and counselor to Louis XVI, who would represent the ill-fated king at his trial in 1792, and who had such "a virtuous and good Heart" that Morris found it "impossible not to feel a very sincere Affection for him." Morris also became a constant visitor at the home of the widow of the Marquis de Chastellux, who had been Rochambeau's chief of staff in America and a friend of Morris. The Marques de Chastellux was an Irish woman in her late twenties who bore her late husband's son not long after Morris arrived. Her circle included the beautiful Duchesse d'Orléans and Madame de Ségur, wife of the Comte (not the previously mentioned Vicomte) de Ségur, who had also served in America. Morris spent many enjoyable hours in the company of these intelligent and lively women.

Morris also made the acquaintance of many of the figures at the center of the political stage, including Jacques Necker, the Swiss-born director of finances. Necker had come to work in Paris as a young clerk and made a fortune by the time he was in his early thirties. Though he had attempted reforms to the inequitable tax system, he was most popular because he pursued a policy of borrowing rather than raising taxes, easing the burden on the taxpayers but driving the country towards bankruptcy. In 1781, he was dismissed from his position at the behest of Marie Antoinette. He thereafter published denunciations of his successor's efforts at reform, and in 1788 he was recalled to the ministry by popular outcry. When Morris met him, he was easily the most admired man in France, but Morris was unimpressed. He thought Necker's financial proposals unworkable, as indeed they would prove to be. "[H]e is one of those people who has obtained a much greater Reputation than he had any Right to," he wrote to Washington. Although Necker's integrity was "unspotted," he continued, "his

Writings on finance teem with that Sort of Sensibility which makes the Fortune of modern Romances, and which is exactly suited to this lively Nation, who love to read but hate to think." Morris was more impressed by the conversation at the famous salon hosted by Necker's famous daughter, Madame de Staël, the brilliant but promiscuous wife of the Swiss ambassador to France. Although he was put off by her masculine appearance, they became friends and discussed politics frequently, albeit rarely agreeing with one another.

Morris also reestablished his friendship with the Marquis de Lafayette, who initially received him with much enthusiasm in the belief that, like Jefferson, Morris would encourage his ambitions both for the country and for himself. Morris soon realized, however, that Lafayette was no more capable than Necker of guiding France safely through a revolution, and his frank criticism and unpalatable suggestions made him a far less welcome visitor to the Lafayette household.

A new friend was the Comte de Montmorin, minister of foreign affairs. He and Morris liked each other immediately, and Montmorin clearly admired and respected Morris's judgment, but the reverse was not true. While Morris grew attached to Montmorin, he commented to Washington that Montmorin "means well, very well. But he means it feebly."

Reform and revolution were the talk of Paris salons in the cold spring of 1789. The country was preparing for the first meeting of the Estates-General in 175 years, a legislative assembly made of representatives from the entire country that had been used by French kings since the fourteenth century to endorse their policies (and the taxes that paid for them). The decision to convene the assemblage had been forced on the king and his ministers as they struggled to find a means of averting national bankruptcy. The country's fiscal affairs had been headed toward disaster for decades, based as they were on a corrupt and inefficient system of tax privileges for the wealthy, well-paid sinecures for the well connected, and an economy strangled by internal customs barriers. French support of the American Revolution had aggravated the situation, as had widespread shortages due to a bad harvest in the summer of 1788. The government was in desperate need of new taxes, but the political climate required that any such effort must involve dismantling the ancient system of privilege.

Louis XVI and his ministers had made several attempts since 1776 to pass reforms, but they had been unable to obtain the required endorsement of the country's quasi-legislative *parlements.* Lafayette, with Jefferson's quiet counsel, had been one of the leaders of the "Patriotic" party, which opposed Necker's predecessor and demanded a statement of accounts. The *parlements* issued protests against the king in 1787 and refused to approve loans for the government, telling him that nothing would be approved until he agreed to call an Estates-General. After an unsuccessful effort to oust the *parlements,* Louis recalled Necker to his position in finances and issued a decree to call the Estates-General to meet in May 1789 at Versailles.

The three "Estates" consisted of elected representatives of the three orders (the nobility, the church, and commoners). Louis's convocation decree left one critical issue undecided: the manner in which the three Estates were to vote on the proposed reforms. At the previous Estates-General, votes had been by "order," with the result that the nobility and clergy—representing a fraction of the country's population and wealth—could always combine to overrule the majority third estate. Faced with increasingly loud demands for reform, Louis and Necker had ordered a doubling of the third estate representatives, but they decided to leave it to the Estates-General to determine whether votes would be by head or by order. The battles over this issue would metamorphose into the start of revolution.

The Estates-General was to consider a constitution and a bill of rights, subjects of enthusiastic interest to the French after the recent publication of the American Constitution. Despite his reservations about the American document, Jefferson had been working with Lafayette on forming a version for the French. Morris wrote to the French minister in London, a friend from the American war, "Republicanism is absolutely a moral Influenza from which neither Titles, Places, nor even the Diadem can guard their Possessor." Morris was never one to trust popular movements, and his new French friends were disconcerted when he responded to their enthusiasm with caution. Although he had "just as it were emerged from that Assembly which has formed one of the most republican of all republican Constitutions," Morris wrote, he found himself "preach[ing] incessantly Respect for the Prince, Attention to the Rights of the Nobility, and Moderation not only in the Object but also in the Pursuit of it."

Morris's frank skepticism about the ability of France to operate under a republican form of government caused many of his new acquaintances to draw back; some, including Madame de Lafayette, labeled him an aristocrat. Yet his observations of France reinforced his distaste for monarchy and the oppressive class structure of French society, and he strongly favored reform. Paris's "[s]plendor is owing entirely to Despotism and must be diminished by the adoption of a better Government," he told Lafayette. He wrote to Robert Morris's wife about a walk he had taken one morning to the top of an aqueduct from which he could see Paris and the Palace of St. Germains and the villages dotted about. To his American eye, though the magnificence of the buildings was undeniable, their coexistence with wretchedly poor villages simply served to underscore the rottenness of the French system. He had, he told her, "exulted in the Consciousness that we [Americans] are Members of a Society which is composed neither of Subjects, nor of Slaves, but of Men." His "most dear" friends in America, he told her, were ones "to whom respect gives rank and with whom virtue is nobility."

Thomas Jefferson took a liking to Morris, inviting him for dinner numerous times and spending time with him sightseeing in Paris. Morris's diary contains the record of many comfortable conversations with Jefferson on a great variety of topics, from politics to viniculture. When Morris was ill in June, Jefferson stopped by to check on him and brought him an American newspaper. By July, Jefferson wrote to his intimate friend Maria Cosway in London that Morris was "his friend" and deserved to be of "great consideration" everywhere. Despite the differences in their personalities, they had similarly cautious views regarding the French Revolution at the outset. Jefferson's perceptions would alter significantly when he returned to the United States, primarily because of political considerations on his side of the Atlantic, while Morris remained consistently pessimistic.

Morris liked Jefferson but was not awed by him. After an evening together, he wrote in his diary that he thought that Jefferson did not "form very just Estimates of Character but rather assigns too many to the humble Rank of Fools." Morris, more charitably and perhaps more realistically, believed that "the Gradations are infinite and each Individual has his peculiarities of Fort and Feeble." Although he had been sent to France to attempt to undo the damage Jefferson had done to Robert's tobacco contracts, Gouverneur wrote to Robert that Jefferson "commands very great Respect in this Country and which is merited by good Sense and good Intentions . . . Mr. Jefferson lives well keeps a good Table and excellent Wines which he distributes freely and by his Hospitality to his Countrymen here possesses very much their good Will."

On May 5, 1789, Morris arose early to take his carriage to Versailles to watch the opening of the Estates-General. He had attended the opening ceremony the day before in the chapel at Versailles. The First Estate led the procession, dressed in scarlet and royal purple; the Second Estate came next in their elaborate court finery; and then the Third Estate in black plain broadcloth. The elaborate costumes and ceremony and the ornate architecture must have presented to Morris a fascinating contrast to the delegates' modest dress and the overheated hall in Philadelphia two years before. On the first meeting day, he listened to speeches by King Louis, Necker, and others for four hours. He emerged unimpressed, though he was touched by the sight of Marie Antoinette's apparent tears in the face of hostility from the crowd.

While the representatives struggled during the next month with the issue of voting by order or by head, Morris deepened his acquaintance with Paris and its society. He was asked by the famous sculptor Houdon, who had made busts of Franklin, Jefferson, and other luminaries, to pose for the body of a sculpture of Washington. Given Morris's wooden leg, it is a testament to what others called Morris's "commanding bearing" that Houdon would make this request. Morris agreed to pose—the sculpture stands today in the capitol rotunda in Richmond, Virginia. Houdon also made a wax impression of Morris's face.

In mid-June, as Morris was coming down with a bad cold, the Estates at Versailles began to transform into a revolutionary body. The parish priests of the First Estate were the first to accept the invitation of the Third Estate to join deliberations on a new constitution, thus abandoning the rest of their order. By June 17 the majority of the First and Second Estates had followed, and the new National Assembly was declared. On June 23, fearing interference by the king, the delegates convened at a nearby indoor tennis court and together took the famous "Tennis Court Oath," swearing to stay in session until a new constitution had been drafted.

Alarmed, the antireform party at court, led by the king's brother, the Comte d'Artois, tried to squelch the new body. Under this party's influence, Louis, who was distracted by the sudden death of his oldest son, ordered the Estates to meet separately. Although he backtracked on June 27, acknowledging the unitary nature of the Assembly, he had in the meantime ordered troops to the vicinity of Paris, raising widespread fears that he would nullify his concessions. By early July, about twenty thousand soldiers were camped outside the city walls.

While Morris kept mostly to his rooms to nurse his cold, the situation worsened rapidly. The price of bread was the highest it had been in a century, and there were food shortages. While at Jefferson's residence for a fourth of July celebration, Morris cornered Lafayette and urged that any constitution would need to accord part of the power to the nobility. Sounding much as he had on the floor of the Constitutional Convention, Morris told Lafayette that this was the "only Means of preserving any Liberty for the People." The French, Morris wrote, "want an American Constitution with the Exception of a King instead of a President, without reflecting that they have not American Citizens to support that Constitution."

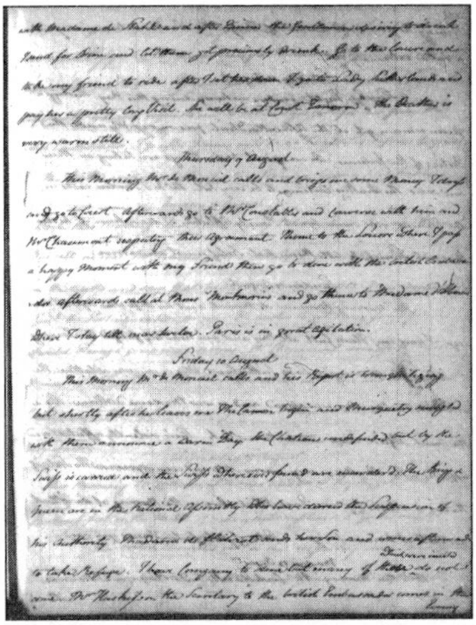

Fig. 7: A page from the volume of Morris's Paris diary at the Library of Congress, showing the beginning of the entry of the fateful day of August 10, 1792, when the Tuileries Palace was attacked and King Louis XVI fell. "The Cannon begin and Musquetry mingled with them announce a warm Day," Morris recorded.

On July 11, Louis made a critical strategic error, dismissing the still-popular Necker. (Apparently no one knew that Necker had seriously considered blowing up the new Assembly's meeting chamber on June 17). When on July 12 the people of Paris learned of Louis's action, the response was immediate and fierce. Morris went to visit a friend at the Louvre, where he learned that Marie Antoinette and the Count d'Artois had been behind the dismissal. The other guests were tense, and Morris offered to escort one of them home. They drove right by a battle between a mob throwing stones and a "Body of Cavalry with their Sabres drawn." Further on, he saw a mob that included members of Lafayette's National Guard breaking into stores to seize arms and munitions. "These poor Fellows have passed the Rubicon with a Witness," he observed. "Success or a Halter must now be their Motto." The next day, the violence increased as mobs roamed the streets to seize "Arms wherever they can find any." On July 14, Morris heard of the takeover of the Bastille, which he considered an "Instance of great Intrepidity," and he concluded that "the whole Conspiracy ag[ainst] Freedom is blown up to the Moon." Jefferson seconded his enthusiasm. One of Morris's acquaintances wrote that night to William Constable: "The Governour and Lt. Governour were put to death and their heads elevated upon long poles, which were carried through the principal streets and exhibited in Palais Royal (which Mr. Govr. Morris very properly calls the Liberty pole of France) before six o'clock this evening. . . ."

Morris's "Liberty pole" comment was not typical of his reactions to the turbulence in Paris. He had not actually *seen* the heads of the governor and lieutenant governor, and when he did see a similar incident he was appalled. A week after the Bastille fell, Morris was waiting for his carriage to pick him up near the Palais Royal when "the Head and Body of Mr. de Foulon are introduced in Triumph. The Head on a Pike, the Body dragged naked on the Earth. Afterwards this horrible Exhibition is carried thro the different Streets. . . . This mutilated Form of an old Man of seventy five is shewn to Bertier, his Son in Law, the Intendt. [administrator] of Paris, and afterwards he also is put to death and cut to Pieces, the Populace carrying about the mangled Fragments with a Savage Joy. Gracious God what a People!" Foulon's mouth had been stuffed with straw, apparently because he was rumored to have said that if the people were hungry, they could eat hay.

Morris got no sleep that night. Just before five in the morning he wrote of what he had seen to Mrs. Robert Morris. "If I should paint to you the Scenes which [illegible] witnessed you would from that Picture alone without further Assurance be convinced of the ardent Desire I feel to return to my native Country," he wrote.

I was never till now fully apprized of the mildness of American character. I have seen my countrymen enraged and threatening. It has even happened that in an affray some Lives were lost. But we know not what it is to slay the defenseless Victim who is in our Power. We cannot parade the Heads of our fellow Citizens and drag the mangled Carcasses through the streets. We cannot feast our Eyes on such Spectacles.

The "Spectacles" had only just begun.

CHAPTER EIGHT

"A PLEASING WOMAN"

IT IS UNSURPRISING THAT GOUVERNEUR MORRIS ADDRESSED his letter about the scene at the Palais Royale to a woman. Morris liked and respected women and his letters to them were generally more revealing than those he wrote to men. His friendships with women gave him access to a rich source of information and political insight concerning the events in France. In this he was quite unlike Jefferson, who believed women should have nothing to do with politics and that many of the problems in France could be traced to their inappropriate influence. Morris felt otherwise. He did not hesitate to discuss business with women, and he sought their political opinions throughout his stay. Though Morris occasionally made humorous references to the role of women in politics, he had as many serious discussions with women as with men during his years in Europe.

Morris was lonely, but he did not expect to find love in France, believing that his heart was "shut up." It took him some time to be facile in idiomatic French and this was a social handicap that made him feel more isolated. Some women flirted with him, including the Duchesse d'Orléans, but he soon realized that they had no real intentions of having a relationship with him.

But love was waiting for Morris in the form of Adélaide Filleul, Comtesse de Flahaut. She was a flower of late-eighteenth-century French society: lovely and highly intelligent, she wrote with a skill that made Morris himself acknowledge inferiority. She had a husband thirty-five years older than she and a young son by her long-time lover, Charles-Maurice de Talleyrand-Périgord (Talleyrand). With a small apartment in the Louvre and a wide circle of friends, she was in the thick of politics and in a position to hear rumor and news as quickly as anyone in Paris.

Adèle's mother had been one of Louis XV's mistresses. Adèle was orphaned when she was six and sent to a convent, where she was mothered by a British nun who taught her English. When she was eighteen, she married Charles de Flahaut, keeper of the king's gardens. Charles and Adèle lived on small pensions from the crown and from the Count d'Artois.

Morris's diary records his immediate interest in Adèle when he met her in March; the fact that she spoke English probably helped. She "is a pleasing Woman. If I might judge from Appearances, not a sworn Enemy to Intrigue." She liked him, too, and asked their hostess to invite him again. Before long, he was paying regular visits to her at the Louvre. He did not seem aware that his interest was turning into something else, though it is obvious from his diary, for on the days he did not find her at home he was unhappy and his mind was "I know not why . . . below its usual Tone." He also took an immediate dislike to Talleyrand, the father of Adèle's seven-year-old son. Morris's first impression of Talleyrand, who was then the Bishop d'Autun, was that he was "sly, cool, cunning, and ambitious." Even if that assessment was born of jealousy, it was remarkably astute, as Talleyrand's long career, during which he moved easily and with frank cynicism to the service of the newest in power, would bear out.

Morris's first impression would be somewhat tempered by his eventual recognition of Talleyrand's considerable intelligence and talents, but he despised his gambling and his apparent aversion to hard work. Adèle and Talleyrand continued to be lovers, though she would claim otherwise to Morris. Talleyrand shared Morris's admiration of Adèle's political insight and often sought her advice.

By late July, Morris was ensnared. Although Adèle told him she had a "marriage of the heart"—meaning Talleyrand—she must have made it clear that she was tempted by Morris, and on July 27 they had sex for the first time. Two days later he left for a business trip to London, but their love affair resumed when he returned a month later. It consumed Morris: they would make love at every opportunity for the next few years, often in circumstances in which they could easily have been discovered. Though much of the explicit detail was blacked out in the 1830s by Morris's widow, Morris's diary records encounters in Adèle's former convent, in his carriage, in Adèle's apartment while her niece was tucked into the window seat reading. He never stayed overnight with her, however; and in company, he wrote, "[a]ppearances are scrupulously observed between us." On the other hand, he was extremely rude to Adèle's husband, who hoped to exploit the connection with Morris, but who also periodically rebelled against his wife's polite indifference and tried to claim his marriage rights—to no avail.

Though he was in love, Morris was uncomfortable with the situation. It seems clear that at least part of Adèle's attraction to

Morris lay in the hope that he might be a source of security for herself and her son. Talleyrand's finances were uncertain, and he apparently did little or nothing to contribute to their support. After a few months with Morris, Adèle briefly suspected that she was pregnant and went so far as to ask him to promise to marry her. Morris recoiled. "[T]his is I know a Business to which there is no End and therefore I refuse." Adèle told him she was in love with him, but he was suspicious of such declarations and believed that passionate love was impermanent. He must also have suspected that, despite her avowals, his attachment to her was stronger than hers to him, and it appears that his often crass efforts to wound her with assumed indifference or to make her jealous were efforts to establish a dominant role and to ensure her continued interest. He hoped that "Anxiety may keep her Passion alive."

Whether Adèle's feelings for Morris were actually enhanced or diminished by these painful strategies is uncertain. She certainly did not relinquish her relationship with Talleyrand, though Morris thought otherwise. "I may if I please wean her from all Regard towards him," he wrote in his diary. "But he is the Father of her Child and it would be unjust." Morris was to suffer much grief when they finally parted, but he apparently never really hesitated in pursuing the affair. Perhaps he thought the incompatibility of their different circumstances would insulate him from true attachment. He was quite wrong about this, at least with respect to himself.

Adèle's apartment was a clearinghouse for news, secret and otherwise, and Morris's relationship with her led to his greater involvement in the Revolution. Talleyrand belonged to the reforming Society of Thirty and Adèle had many friends at court, including Viq d'Azyr, the Queen's personal physician and counselor. She introduced Morris to her circle, and he talked politics with all of them.

Morris's gradual entanglement in French affairs may also have been influenced by his observation of Jefferson's activities during the summer of 1789. Unlike Jefferson, Morris was in France as a private citizen; like Jefferson, he wanted to help the reforms succeed. Once started, however, he would find it very difficult to stop. "The love of order is his strongest passion, the rule of all his acts, the aim of all he utters," wrote one of Morris's French friends a few years later. "A true philanthropist by the natural impulse of his soul, he considers every object under the possibility of its becoming useful."

Before he departed for London in August, Morris had prepared a memorandum on constitutional issues at the request of the new Assembly's constitutional committee. His comments could not have been welcome to the reformers. France was not ready for a free government, he told them flatly; the individual Estates should be preserved in order to keep control of the most powerful parts of society or the proposed constitution would fail. The arguments were essentially the same as those he had made at Philadelphia but reflected his observations of the very different society of France.

He had watched the Assembly in action and found the men extremely disorderly. They "neither reason examine nor discuss," he wrote to Robert. "They clap those whom they approve and hiss those whom they disapprove." He told the president of the Assembly that it was "impossible for such a Mob to govern this Country. . . . [T]he executive Authority is reduced to a Name. Everything almost is elective and consequently Nobody obeys." He told Robert that the French intellectuals, who were out of touch with reality, had "turned the Heads of their Countrymen and they have run amuck [at] a Don Quixote Constitution." "You will judge," he added, "the Effects of such a Constitution upon a People supremely depraved. They are devilish wicked—"

But the tide of the Revolution was inexorable. On his return from London, Morris learned to his dismay that the Assembly had decided to give the king only a temporary veto and to have a single legislature. On August 4, at Lafayette's initiative, the nobility in the Assembly had renounced the privileges they had held for centuries. On August 26, the Assembly adopted the famous *Declaration of the Rights of Man and Citizen.*

Jefferson, though he would later claim that his sense of propriety as a diplomat had kept him detached, was heavily involved with these developments. One American observer wrote on the very evening a major constitutional discussion took place at Jefferson's residence that Jefferson was "to this revolution what a key and main Spring are to a watch. He winds them up & puts them into motion."

In the meantime, Paris was growing increasingly agitated. Bread was ever more expensive and the people were growing angry with what they perceived to be the slow pace of the Assembly and the intransigence of the king, who had not sanctioned any of the Assembly's decrees. Morris talked to Necker and Lafayette about importing flour, but Lafayette was uninterested. Morris wrote angrily that Lafayette was "very much below the Business he has undertaken" and that "if the Sea runs high he will be unable to hold the helm." Necker was no better: "[H]e treats the Idea of Responsibility of the Nation for such Use of public Money with Contempt," Morris recorded with disbelief.

As the situation grew more ominous, Morris's advice to Lafayette grew more trenchant and undoubtedly less welcome. Lafayette was the head of the National Guard, a seemingly powerful position, but Morris saw that Lafayette did not have control of his troops. On October 1, with remarkable prescience, he warned

Lafayette that he must regain command, because "if the People of this Metropolis want, they will send their Leaders to the Devil at once and ask again their Bread and their Chains."

A few days later came the frightening October Days: rumors of a royalist plot against the August reforms had swept Paris, and Lafayette's National Guard demanded to go to Versailles to "protect" Louis from "conspirators." They were led by throngs of angry women singing satirical songs about the king and demanding bread. Lafayette tried to keep his troops in Paris but had to give in. Morris and the others then at Adèle's apartment were taken aback by the news. "Lafayette has marched by Compulsion, guarded by his own Troops who suspect and threaten him," Morris recorded in his diary. Louis and his family were forced by the crowds to return to Paris under the escort of Lafayette, where they took up what was effectively house arrest in the Tuileries Palace. "[U]nfortunate Prince!" Morris wrote." The Victim of his Weakness, and in the Hands of those who are not to be relied on even for Pity. What a dreadful Lesson it is for Man that an absolute Prince cannot with Safety be indulgent. The Troubles of this Country are begun, but as to the End it is not easy to foresee it."

Though Morris and others recognized the October Days as proof of Lafayette's weakness, his celebrity soared while the king's fell, and for a while he seemed to be the most powerful man in France, able to choose ministers and dictate policy. Seeing clearly that the king's lack of talented administrators might be fatal to the monarchy, Morris worried that Lafayette would not make wise decisions. "I consider the present time as critical," Morris told Lafayette, "[and] that if neglected many inseparable mischiefs must pursue." Adèle did not miss the opportunity to promote Talleyrand as a potential replacement for Necker, and Morris agreed to recommend him, believing Talleyrand more capable than Necker (not to mention the fact that he would have been a better contact for Morris's commercial ventures).

Lafayette had his own ideas about whom to nominate, however. Among his candidates was the notorious Comte de Mirabeau, well known for his venality and immorality. Morris was shocked that Lafayette would consider Mirabeau, but the canny count knew how to flatter Lafayette. He staged a demonstration of public support at the National Assembly and gave a speech calling Lafayette a "sage, whom only an interest in humanity called to the fields of glory," which moved Lafayette to tears. Privately, however, Mirabeau commented that if the public "knew the sort of ministry without responsibility [Lafayette] wished to arrogate to himself, his public credit would be ruined." Morris would have agreed with this remark, if reluctantly. He observed in his diary that Lafayette had a "vaulting Ambition which o'erleaps itself. The Man's Mind is so elated by Power, already too great for the Measure of his Abilities, that he looks in to the Clouds and grasps at the Supreme." "From this Moment," Morris predicted sadly, but accurately, "every Step in his Ascent will I think accelerate his Fall."

Morris also gave Lafayette stern advice on the defects of the draft constitution, objecting first and foremost to putting the king's executive authority at the mercy of the legislature, which could impeach his ministers. Lafayette claimed to have followed some of Morris's recommendations but in fact did nothing, and at one point he told the astonished Morris that even if it had defects he "must acknowlege that their Constitution is better than that of England." Morris flatly disagreed. His condemnation was justified, for the Constitution of 1791, as it would be called, proved unworkable and was eventually universally rejected

The bread shortage continued. Just two days after Lafayette was fêted by Mirabeau, a baker accused of hoarding bread was beheaded by a man in a National Guard uniform. The head was paraded through the streets. "Surely it is not in the usual Order of divine Providence to leave such Abominations unpunished," Morris wrote in his diary, dismayed. "The Pressure of incumbent Despotism is removed, every bad Passion exerts its peculiar Energy."

Morris also found little encouragement in the government's attempts to salvage the country's finances. He wrote Washington that the government was only hanging on by borrowing, and that Necker's ideas were impractical and even absurd, such as asking the citizens to pay a voluntary "patriotic" tax of about one quarter of their income. The Catholic Church, long resented for its huge assets and the protection of its ancient privileges, was also seen as a way of solving the country's financial woes. Though no admirer of Catholicism, Morris opposed the proposal (later adopted) to make church officials subject to the civil government instead of the pope. He believed that religion was "the only solid Base of Morals and that Morals are the only possible Support of free Governments." When the church lands were nationalized along with lands belonging to the crown, they were used as a basis to issue paper *assignats* secured by the land, an idea he considered dangerous. "The dreadful primordial Curse is repeated upon them all," he wrote to William Short, who was the interim *chargé des affaires* after Jefferson left for America. "Paper thou art and unto Paper thou shalt return." The *assignats* began to depreciate almost immediately, as Morris, who had seen too much of paper currency during the American Revolution, had predicted they would.

The government's financial crisis was of interest to Morris not only because of its impact on the course of the Revolution but because it concerned the American Revolutionary War debt to France, one of his primary business assignments while in France. He devoted much of his time during his first year in Europe attempting to persuade Necker and others in the French government to agree to sell the debt to the group he represented. The issues presented by the debt are complex but deserve a brief explanation so as to give the reader an idea of one of the biggest investment attractions of the day.

America's unsettled finances in the postwar Confederation era had caused it to stop payments on the 35 million *livres* it owed to the French, beginning in 1785. The adoption of the Constitution in 1789 greatly improved America's standing as a credit risk, for it meant the government would be able to raise loans and revenue to repay the debt. However, Alexander Hamilton, the new secretary of the treasury, asked the French if they would be willing to defer collection of the principal for a few years while the domestic war debt was addressed. France's financial straits made this an unpalatable suggestion, and investors, including the Morrises, suggested that a better solution was to help France by proposing a reduced repayment immediately, with the investors to take a profit by receiving the eventual full repayment from the United States.

It was a large-scale, unusual proposal, but it was made by some of the day's most knowledgeable financiers. While adoption of this approach meant that France would not receive its repayment in full, America was not in a position to make *any* significant payments immediately, and France was in urgent need of money. Some, like Jefferson, who seemed unaware that a large proportion of the American domestic debt had been purchased by European speculators, proclaimed their aversion to the idea of putting American obligations in private hands. Jefferson preferred the expedient of raising Dutch loans, which was not possible prior to the adoption of the Constitution and which would still take considerable time even after it was ratified.

There was an additional element that complicated the matter: the depreciation of the French *livre,* a decline that had already begun when Morris arrived in France. If taken advantage of by the speculators *or* by the United States, this factor would further reduce the net repayment to the French.

The stakes were high and there was fierce competition among the speculators to sign Necker on to their proposals. The Frenchman Brissot de Warville, who would play a pivotal role in the Girondin party period of the French Revolution, led a group that included numerous Americans. They were unsuccessful, and it is likely that their competition with the Morris group was the root of Brissot's later extreme dislike of Morris. One of Brissot's associates was Etienne Clavière, a Swiss banker who would become the Girondin minister of finance and whose corruption would become notorious. Daniel Parker, an occasional business partner of the Morrises and an appealing scallywag who would cause Morris many headaches in the next few years, initially worked with Brissot but deserted him to join with Morris. The desperate financial situation made the speculators' proposals attractive to Necker, and Morris worked hard during the summer and fall of 1789 to reach an agreement, at Necker's request consenting to work with Dutch bankers in finalizing an arrangement. The Dutch bankers, however, were loath to give up the large—and risk-free—commissions that raising loans for the U.S. to pay off the debt would yield. In January 1790, without advance approval, the Dutch houses issued a 3 million florin loan on behalf of the United States and wrote to Hamilton for his endorsement, which he gave. Morris felt betrayed and frustrated by the bankers, because he predicted, rightly, that Hamilton would put most of the money to domestic uses, further delaying any relief for the French. The French would not receive full repayment for nearly five years, something Morris's proposals would have avoided.

Morris temporarily gave up on the debt purchase for much of the next year, for he was away from France and working for Washington in attempted negotiations with the British (to be discussed in the next chapter). When he was notified in March 1791 that the American government considered his mission completed, he returned to the debt. This time, another group of speculators, the Paris bankers Schweizer and Jeanneret, was seeking his participation through James Swan, a frequent business partner with Morris in his European ventures. Morris's share was to be payment for his services in persuading the French and the United States governments to agree to terms. He recommended the proposal to William Short, and did the same in a letter to George Washington. He told neither man of his personal involvement, however, apparently to preserve the illusion of objectivity; though he wrote in his diary that it was his "sincere belief" that it was a good plan for the United States, this was not one of Morris's finest moments.

The plan failed, however, because it appealed to neither Jefferson nor Hamilton. They wanted America to take advantage of the depreciation of French money, and Jefferson also wanted to use the repayments as leverage to extract trading concessions from the French. Yet the use of depreciated money meant that France would get far less than it had given the United States, and the decision to raise European loans for repayments meant even greater delays in what France did finally receive. It is therefore difficult to say that anyone on the American side deserves much credit for the handling of the repayment of what had been for America the saving financial support for its Revolution. As representatives of the United States, Jefferson and Hamilton sought only the American advantage; as the representative of private investors, Morris sought a private advantage that he also thought was in the best interests of France.

It was not until 1794, when the king who had approved the original loans to America had been dead for over a year, that the majority of the loan was repaid. James Swan got approval from the American government to convert the remainder into domestic bonds, which he used to buy supplies for the French military.

CHAPTER NINE

LONDON

WHILE THE NATIONAL ASSEMBLY CONTINUED WORK ON A constitution and Necker struggled with the financial crisis, Paris was uneasy. As Gouverneur Morris had warned Lafayette, the political and financial situation, coupled with the abdication of the privileges of the nobility in August 1789 and the National Assembly's stoppage of payments to pensioners of the crown, drove many of the former nobles and well-to-do from France. Would-be émigrés to the United States began to visit Morris to talk about purchasing American lands. In mid-January 1790, there were riots in Paris, and peasants burned chateaux throughout the country. King Louis XVI tried to reassert his authority by formally declaring himself the "head of the Revolution" at a meeting of the National Assembly in February, but the resulting uptick in royal popularity was brief. While Morris was in London from February to October, Louis's power diminished steadily, as the beleaguered monarch was forced to make repeated concessions to the Assembly.

Morris watched these developments with concern, but he was distracted from the situation in France for much of the following year. In late January, he received a letter from George Washington asking him to talk to the British about completion of the 1783 peace treaty terms. Washington wanted to have the contact made "informally, by a private agent." The British had continued to hold army posts in what was then the northwestern United States (including Detroit, Oswego, Niagara, and elsewhere), and had not paid compensation for slaves freed by British troops, both contrary to the treaty. On their side, the American state governments had not met their obligation to enforce repayment by American citizens of money owed to British lenders before the war began.

Washington left it up to Morris to decide whether to discuss the issue of exchanging ministers. The British had studiously ignored John Adams when he was posted to London a few years earlier and had yet to send a minister to America; Adams had finally been recalled rather than continue to suffer what was felt to be a national insult. President Washington also directed Morris to inquire what the British would need for a commercial treaty between the countries to be achieved. He emphasized the importance of obtaining an accurate judgment of British intentions, and that the effort should "receive every advantage, which abilities, address, and delicacy can promise and afford."

Morris's mission to London would have long-lasting repercussions for his career. Washington clearly considered Morris to have the necessary "abilities, address, and delicacy," and Morris would acquit himself brilliantly in his talks with the British. However, thanks in large part to his old friend Alexander Hamilton, many in America believed—and many historians still believe—that Gouverneur Morris bungled the mission and worsened Anglo-American relations. For when Morris reported Britain's indifference to the American approach, Hamilton deliberately undermined Morris and manipulated Washington in an attempt to salvage his paramount goal, an Anglo-American commercial treaty.

Morris did not leave for London for nearly a month after he heard from Washington. He was still hoping to save the debt purchase with the Dutch, and apparently he did not want to leave Adèle. There was again reason to think she might be pregnant, and he hoped it was true, thinking it would strengthen their attachment. She was not, and during the eight months of his absence she would draw away from him.

After stopping in Amsterdam in a fruitless effort to convince the Dutch bankers to make good on the debt agreement, Morris arrived in London on March 27, 1790. Two days later, he met with the British foreign secretary, the Duke of Leeds, at Whitehall. Leeds had been expecting him, although Morris didn't know it—the British agent Major George Beckwith had been detailed to scout out the doings of the American government in New York and had reported Morris's mission.

Leeds seemed receptive, but when Morris raised specific issues concerning the peace treaty it became clear that the foreign secretary could only make assurances of goodwill. The British were secretly attempting to lure Vermont and Kentucky away from the United States by offers of commercial treaties, and they had no interest in evacuating the northwestern forts or in concluding a commercial treaty with the U.S. government. Leeds told Morris that they intended to send a minister to America but had found no suitable candidate. After that, nothing more remaining to be said, they parted. Leeds promised to be in touch with Morris shortly, but he had no intention of doing so.

Morris was not surprised. As he reported to Washington, their old wartime friend, the Chevalier de La Luzerne, now French minister to London, warned him to expect nothing from Britain. When a month passed with no word from Leeds, Morris concluded that the British government was not going to respond. They were not willing to say so directly, he told Washington, but would instead "color their breach of faith by the best pretexts in their power." It was, Morris said, a bad time to negotiate, because "Perhaps there never was a moment in which this country [Britain] felt herself greater." This conclusion was confirmed to Morris by Charles Fox, the famous opposition leader. Morris met Fox at the home of Alexander Hamilton's lovely sister-in-law, Angelica Schuyler Church, where Morris was a frequent visitor.

Quite unexpectedly, however, the British attitude changed. In early May, news came that Britain had demanded satisfaction from Spain for the capture of several British ships off of Vancouver, in Nootka Sound, an incident that had occurred a year earlier. War seemed imminent, and the prospect made the English far more interested in a rapprochement with the United States for strategic reasons.

Morris was surprised by the British decision to confront Spain. As he later put it to Leeds:

> [A]t first I did suppose it might excite some Alteration between the two Nations, but recollecting that no british Subject could be in those Seas without the express Permission of the India Company, and presuming from the whole View of the Transaction that these Adventurers had not that Permission, I concluded that no Notice would be taken of the Matter, because that Spain might have sent them all to England in Irons as having been taken in the direct Violation of a british Act of Parliament, and

in such Case, my Lord, I don't see how you could have done otherwise than have thanked the King of Spain for so kind and brotherly a Proceedure.*

As Morris suggested to Washington, however, the demand was a deliberate move by Britain undertaken to challenge Spanish domination of the Pacific coast—and it would succeed.

The scramble to prepare for possible war led to an immediate "hot Press"—impressments of men into the British navy—and Morris soon learned that the sweep had caught up American sailors as well. Thomas Paine, who was living in London, and John Brown Cutting, a friend of Jefferson, asked Morris to make a protest to the ministry of defense. Morris was uneasy about exceeding his instructions, but he requested a meeting and in the third week of May he met again with Leeds. On the second day of talks, the brilliant prime minister William Pitt joined them. The conversation, which Morris recorded in his diary, makes entertaining reading. The British were at this point very worried that the United States would support Spain through France in the war that was brewing. To forestall this, they told Morris that they were now interested in a possible commercial treaty. Morris immediately discerned their motives and told them that a new treaty would be "idle" until the peace treaty was satisfied. He then turned the discussion to American concerns. "As to the compensation for negroes taken away," he told Pitt, "it is too trifling an object for you to dispute, so that nothing remains but the posts; I suppose, therefore, that you wish to retain these posts." He went on: "They are not worth the keeping, for it must cost you a great deal of money, and pro-

---

* An entertaining example of Morris's mastery of these conversations. The ships did indeed belong to a subsidiary of the British East India Company.

duce no benefit. The only reason you can have to desire them, is to secure the fur trade, and that will centre in this country, let who will carry it on in America. " The northwest posts, he said, were essential for America to preserve a boundary that would allow the U.S. and Britain to "live in amity," but more than that, they involved national honor. The "conduct you have pursued," he told Pitt, "naturally excites resentment in every American bosom. We do not think it worth while to go to war with you for these posts; but *we know our rights, and will avail ourselves of them, when time and circumstances may suit."*

Pitt suggested that America should be awarding "particular privileges" to Britain for ones given to America, but Morris fired back.

> I assured him that I knew of none, except that of being impressed, a privilege which of all others we least wished to partake of.
>
> The Duke of Leeds observed, in the same style of jocularity, that we were at least treated in that respect as the most favored nation, seeing that we were treated like themselves. But Mr. Pitt said seriously, that they had certainly evidenced good will towards us, by what they had done respecting our commerce. I replied, therefore, with like seriousness, that their regulations had been dictated by a view to their own interest; and therefore, as we felt no favor, we owed no obligation.

Morris's refusal to be obsequious to the British was intentional, though it would distress Hamilton. Gouverneur later explained his strategy to Robert Morris:

> If you mean to make a good Treaty with Britain support your Pretensions with Spirit *and they will respect you for it.* You must give them *visible Reasons* because they will have to *justify their*

Conduct: and it will not do to say to a House of Commons *the American Minster was such a charming fellow that we could not resist him.* I rather think that it would be at least as good ground to say *the American Legislature would have greatly injured our Navigation and Commerce if we had not by this Treaty have induced them to repeal their Laws, and there was Reason also to apprehend that the United States would connect themselves still more intimately with France.*

Washington and Jefferson were pleased with Morris's conduct of the talks. Although the British encouragement to Morris at the May meetings raised American hopes for an imminent resolution to their complaints, Spain's decision to concede to the British spelled the end of those hopes. Morris waited throughout the summer to hear again from the ministry, but as it became clear that Spain did not have the stomach for war, he predicted, correctly, that Britain would offer America nothing.

Alexander Hamilton could not accept this outcome. The secretary of the treasury was determined to have America and Britain form strong commercial ties now that the war was over, and he decided to take matters into his own hands. He tried to get George Washington to offer propitiation to the British by telling him that they had been offended by Morris's behavior, a fabrication he shored up by telling the British agent in New York, George Beckwith—falsely—that the American government was unhappy with Morris.

Hamilton also falsely told Washington that Beckwith had told him the British were interested in both a commercial treaty and a possible military alliance, although Beckwith had told Hamilton the British wanted neither. He also told Washington that the British had objected to Morris's lack of regular diplomatic credentials, which they had not. This supposed objection infuriated Washington, who wrote a blistering comment in his diary that the British attitude

> was simply and no other than this; We [Great Britain] did not incline to give any satisfactory answer to Mr. Morris, who was *officially* commissioned to ascertain our intentions with respect to the evacuation of the Western Posts . . . and other matters into which he was empowered to enquire until by this unauthenticated mode we can discover whether you will enter into an alliance with us and make Common cause against Spain. In that case we will enter into a Commercial Treaty with you and *promise perhaps* to fulfil what they already stand engaged to perform.

Hamilton also told Beckwith that Morris had undoubtedly aggravated the British by an indiscreet friendship with the opposition party in London, implying, falsely, that Morris had spent much time with Fox. Since Morris had reported his only meeting with Fox—at a party held by Hamilton's sister-in-law—this was an outrageous assertion.

A few months later, Washington and Jefferson gave Congress excerpts of Morris's reports in order to gain support for legislation sponsored by James Madison to impose tariffs and other restrictions on British shipping. The British were alarmed and sent Beckwith to talk to Hamilton. This time Beckwith parroted Hamilton's earlier criticisms of Morris, and Hamilton passed his remarks on to Washington, embellishing them to include Morris's supposed "intimacy" with the opposition and an assertion that Morris had alienated the British to the point that they did not wish to deal with him, which was not true.

Hamilton—or Beckwith, or both—must have spread these comments about in Congress, because when Morris's nomination as a minister to France was debated nearly two years later, one senator wrote in his journal of "the disappointment attending Gouverneur Morris's management" of the negotiation, and Aaron Burr took the floor to declare: "I merely state a fact. It has been asserted and without any injunction of secresy, that Mr. Morris conducted himself so offensively in his intercourse with the Eng. Ministers, that they were offended [and] refused, after an abrupt breaking up of an interview, to renew it."

The record shows, however, that Morris's reports were quite accurate and, moreover, that the British were not at all offended by Morris—indeed, he and Lord Grenville, successor to the Duke of Leeds as foreign secretary, had several meetings and corresponded after Morris left France some years later.

When Morris heard of these supposed complaints about him he was disdainful: "I will suppose it to be a very good Reason to be given to America for not conferring *a favor* on her that the Man sent to ask it was disagreable, no matter from what Cause, but I trust that they will never avow to the british Nation a Disposition to make Sacrifice of their Interest to please a pleasant Fellow."

Washington had no reason to disbelieve Hamilton, however. Though he remained Morris's stout friend and would soon name him to a diplomatic post, he was so concerned by Hamilton's allegations that he assigned Morris to Paris, not London, and he accompanied news of the appointment with a cautionary letter to Morris that described the complaints. The letter wounded Morris considerably; he would never learn that the source of the charges was his old friend Hamilton.

But however admirable Morris's handling of his negotiations in London had been, he might well have deserved rebuke from Washington if the president had known of his concurrent efforts to encourage Spain into war, and France into war beside her, against Britain. True, Morris thought that France would merely be preempting a likely attack by the British, and at this time he believed that a state of war was the best hope of restoring central authority to the unraveling nation. He also thought it would push Britain into treaty with America—and, it should be added, give him and his American associates commercial opportunities inevitably associated with war.

Morris did not tell his government what he was up to, although he did tell Washington that he had advised Montmorin that the French should contain their Revolution by "making war abroad." He gave Lafayette suggestions for military strategy and made recommendations to the Spanish ambassador on harassing British commerce in the event of war. However, though the Comte de Montmorin promised Spain that France would honor their compact, he could not follow through; the National Assembly was now gaining power and voted to take over much of the control of foreign affairs, further crippling King Louis.

Morris was ready to abandon London by early July 1790, but he came down with an undisclosed ailment that kept him indoors for the next two months. When he recovered, he wrote again to Leeds, and they met on September 15. Leeds assured Morris that a minister would be sent to America "soon" but would go no further, and Morris saw there was nothing to be gained by further discussions. This was not his last communication with Leeds, however. Impressments of American sailors had continued and at the urgent request of American captains he sent Leeds an incisive letter of protest that made it devastatingly clear that Britain was violating international law. Leeds made no answer, probably because there was none he could make. Britain knew she was strong enough to do as she pleased, legal niceties not withstanding. The matter would continue unresolved and would help precipitate the War of 1812.

In mid-December, having received all of his reports, Washington and Jefferson also concluded that further discussions were futile and instructed Morris to abandon the effort. In February, after extracts of Morris's dispatches went to Congress, the Senate approved Madison's navigation bill. Ironically, this use of Morris's reports of British recalcitrance caused the British to finally appoint a minister to America, a genuine diplomatic breakthrough.

Hamilton, however, refused to give up. Without Washington's or Jefferson's knowledge or permission, he sent John Adams's ambitious and self-important son-in-law, William Stephens Smith, to meet with the British government. In stark contrast to Morris, Smith was extremely propitiating and made no headway with the uninterested ministers. Still, he concluded that it was thanks to him that the British had decided to appoint a minister to America. Smith returned to America and went to see Washington, expecting gratitude, but Washington told Smith flatly that he had told him nothing that he had not already known from Morris. Jefferson agreed; in August 1791, he wrote a letter to Morris to endorse and praise his conduct of the mission, signing it "Your affectionate humble servant."

CHAPTER TEN

RETURN TO PARIS

GOUVERNEUR MORRIS LEFT LONDON IN THE THIRD WEEK of September 1790 and began a six-week trip through Flanders, the Netherlands, and along the Rhine from Cologne to Strasburg, trying unsuccessfully to make American land sales to investors he was introduced to along the way. On November 6, he returned to Paris and hurried to see Adèle. He was brought up short by the discovery of the handsome, young, and wealthy Lord Henry Wycombe at her apartment. Adèle did not help matters by telling him that she still wanted friendship but no sexual relationship. He was devastated. Over the next few weeks they quarreled, and although they did rekindle their physical relationship it was obvious to Morris that Wycombe and Talleyrand were also sleeping with Adèle. "My Bosom is torn with Anxiety and I find in my left Arm as well as in my left Breast a phisical Sense of Grief," he wrote in his diary on December 2.

His misery increased when, a few days later, he received news that his untrustworthy associate Daniel Parker had defaulted on bills to the tune of fifteen thousand pounds, having pilfered the money for personal debts. Adèle burst into tears at Morris's obvious distress and offered him "all the Money" she had, which was some consolation after their unhappy quarreling. Morris left for London immediately and for the next month worked with angry creditors, finally bringing them to a settlement. As soon as the creditors' signatures were on the page, he was off in a mad dash to return to Paris and Adèle. The weather in the Channel was bad and the boat he hired nearly foundered, but the crossing took only three hours and he arrived at Paris at six in the morning. He slept for three hours and then went to Adèle's apartment.

They made love, although a visitor came in "so abruptly as to derange our closing moment." Although he had clearly missed her terribly while in London, it seems that he decided to pursue a strategy of emotional withdrawal, saying to himself in his diary that "the Pain arising from the Apprehension of loosing a Lover is essential to the Pleasure a Woman finds in possessing him." (In the next breath, the candid Morris admitted that the same was true of men.) Thereafter, he followed the advice of his friend Madame de Bourg, who must have perceived his misery, "to pursue rather the *Attraits* [charms] *of Society* than any serious Attachment." He worked, occasionally successfully, to seduce other women of his circle, but he did not manage to detach himself from Adèle. She was "sad," as Morris noted repeatedly in this period, and much of it undoubtedly had to do with anxiety concerning her financial situation—something that probably made the rich Wycombe even more appealing. In May the Flahauts' income from the crown disappeared, and Adèle's hope of becoming one of the queen's ladies, which Morris attempted to promote, did not materialize.

While Morris had been in London, the power of the French monarchy had eroded drastically. The National Assembly had instituted the Civil Constitution of the Clergy, taking over administration of religious clerics from the Catholic Church and establishing elections of clergy by the people. This single act, which Talleyrand (who pretended in public to endorse it) called the Assembly's "greatest political blunder," would alienate many of the religious French, especially outside of Paris. When the clergy resisted it, the National Assembly's successor, the Constituent Assembly, instituted the "Oath of the Civil Constitution" in November 1790—failure to toe the line by taking the oath meant forfeiting one's position. King Louis, who opposed these moves, nonetheless tried to obtain papal approval for them, but the pope denounced the Civil Constitution. From that moment, civil war became inevitable. Necker had resigned in protest over a plan to issue another round of *assignats*. Many believed that the king's brothers, now out of France, would join with other countries to invade France and seize power.

Morris painted a bleak picture of the situation in an eloquent letter to George Washington in November 1790. "This unhappy country, bewildered in the pursuit of metaphysical whimsies, presents to our moral view a mighty ruin," he began.

> Daws and ravens, and the birds of night, now build their nests in its niches. The sovereign, humbled to the level of a beggar's pity, without resources, without authority, without a friend. The Assembly at once a master and a slave, new in power, wild in theory, raw in practice. It engrosses all functions though incapable of exercising any, and has taken from this fierce ferocious people

every restraint of religion and of respect. Sole executors of the law, and therefore supreme judges of its propriety, each district measures out its obedience by its wishes, and the great interests of the whole, split up into fractional morsels, depend on momentary impulse and ignorant caprice.

"Such a state of things cannot last," Morris predicted. "But how will it end? Here conjecture may wander through unbounded space. What sum of misery may be requisite to change popular will, calculation cannot determine. . . . One thing only seems to be tolerably ascertained, that the glorious opportunity is lost, and (for this time at least) the revolution has failed."

Yet Morris was no reactionary. Much as he disapproved of the course of the Revolution, he praised to Washington what he identified as its positive aspects, including the abolition of the crippling system of tax collection that had stultified commerce, and the abolition of feudal privileges, which he called "tyranny," a change that made possible simple and rational ownership rights in property. Though he condemned their use for *assignats,* he approved the nationalization of church lands, for the church's ownership had "damped the ardor of industry." Finally, he endorsed the destruction of the local *parlements,* whose laws he called "venal jurisprudence" and which had "established the pride and privileges of the few on the misery and degradation of the general mass." All of these actions, he said, gave hope for future prosperity, as did "the promulgation and extension of those principles of liberty which will I hope remain to cheer the heart and cherish a nobleness of soul when the metaphysical froth and vapor shall have been blown away," and which might, he thought, eventually induce the leaders of France "to give to this people a real constitution of government fitted to the natural, moral, social, and political state of their country."

On the evening of June 20, 1791, the royal family left the Tuileries Palace one at a time, trying to avoid notice, and climbed aboard a carriage, heading for a rendezvous with one of the French generals and his army. Louis hoped to forestall an attack on France by the other European powers and to retrieve his authority from the Constituent Assembly. The royal family managed to get out of Paris, but its hopes ended when its members were recognized by a postmaster in the village of Varennes. The National Guard took custody of them and they were returned to Paris, the people standing in silence along the roads.

Morris thought the attempted escape "very foolish." He thought Louis should have just sat quiet for a while longer, "because the Anarchy which prevails would have shewn the Necessity of conferring more Authority." Instead, the attempted escape stripped Louis of the last vestiges of public confidence. Though he had rejected and distrusted the offers of foreign and émigré help (at the same time Marie Antoinette was soliciting them), most of the French now concluded that Louis was in league with the foreign courts. He would still make efforts to exert his authority through vetoes, but he became largely irrelevant except as a symbol.

The flight to Varennes "changed every Thing," Morris wrote, "and now the general Wish seems to be for a Republic." On July 17, members of the radical Cordeliers Club went to the fields of the Champs de Mars in Paris to gather signatures for a petition demanding a republic. The crowd grew fractious, and the mayor sent Lafayette and his troops to restore order. Hearing of the confrontation, Morris called for his carriage and drove with Adèle to a nearby hill for a better view, but the explosion had already taken place. The militia, fired upon, had responded with a volley that left about fifty dead. Though the slain were instantly made the martyrs of the "Champs de Mars massacre," Morris's sympathies were with the vastly outnumbered militia who had been required to be "paraded thro the Streets under a scorching Sun and then stand like Holiday Turkeys to be knocked down by Brick-Bats."

The violence of the July 17, 1791, confrontation sobered the radicals for a while. Morris began to hope that intelligent strategy might return order to the country and authority to Louis. He began writing a speech for the king to give when accepting the new constitution, now nearly complete. Morris considered the constitution to be utterly incapable of governing the country, an opinion secretly shared by many—including Brissot de Warville, the anti-monarchical Girondin party leader—and one that would be vindicated in short order. However, for Louis simply to reject the constitution would pulverize his small remaining stock of credibility. Rather, Morris reasoned, he should accept it while simultaneously pointing out its defects very clearly, so that when the constitution was put into effect and began to malfunction, the people would turn to the king.

The problems with the constitution were patently obvious to a man who had helped design constitutions: it lacked the structure of checks and balances that could make a body politic stand upright and walk. Instead, the document opened the door for the Assembly to assume all power—legislative, judicial, and executive. And if, as Morris considered inevitable, a faction gained dominance in the Assembly, there was no built-in means of correction. The king's limited powers were undercut and therefore ineffective.

Morris spelled out these deficiencies in clear language in the proposed speech. He also suggested that the king should begin the speech by calling himself a "citizen" who was now being "offered" his crown back under the conditions described in the constitution. This was too much for men raised in the tradition of reverence for the court, including Montmorin, who was supposed to present Morris's draft to the king. In a move that seems to have been typical of the French court's modus operandi, Montmorin told Morris that the king had found the draft "too forcible"—but Morris did not discover that Montmorin had not actually given the document to Louis until after the king's speech had already been made. The king's advisors had "neither the Sense nor the Spirit the Occasion calls for," Morris wrote in disgust to President Washington on the last day of September 1791. "It is a general and almost universal Conviction that this Constitution is inexecutable. The Makers to a Man condemn it."

Yet Louis must have eventually received Morris's proposed speech and its cover memorandum, and it appears that he took them under advisement. One of the king's counselors recorded remarks by Louis that mirrored Morris's recommendation that he obey the constitution literally and thereby clearly demonstrate its defects. A few weeks later, Morris heard that he "stood high" in the king and queen's opinion.

Unfortunately for Morris, however, many others also came to hear of his efforts. The proponents of the constitution were outraged that Morris had dared to criticize it. In early October one of the Paris newspapers excoriated Morris for his "vain insolence" and "intolerable aristocracy." Even when the constitution had been tossed aside—less than a year later—Morris's enemies would use his "presumption" in criticizing the document as a weapon against him. Yet Morris's efforts for the king continued unabated.

The new constitution called for election of a new legislature, the "Legislative Assembly," which opened at the beginning of October 1791 in an atmosphere of increasing international tension. The German princes who had lost their feudal entitlements had turned to the Austrian emperor for assistance, and their complaints and the urgings of Louis's émigré brothers had led to the Declaration of Pillnitz, issued in August 1791 by the King of Prussia and the emperor. It called for the restoration of Louis XVI's authority and threatened retaliatory steps. Louis was enraged by the declaration. No one, he wrote to his brothers, would ever believe that he had not encouraged it. "[Y]ou portray me to the Nation as accepting [the constitution] with one hand and soliciting [intervention] from the Foreign Powers with the other."

His analysis was depressingly accurate. Led by the persuasive Brissot de Warville, the Girondins were increasingly powerful in the Assembly. (The Girondins were not as fanatical as their later enemies, the Montagnards. They were eager for republican reforms and wanted Louis to be weak and under their control, but there were many lawyers, journalists, and intellectuals in their ranks and they did not want mob rule.) Brissot insistently advocated confrontation with the king at every turn; and at every turn, Louis lost more authority. The Girondins pushed for decrees punishing émigrés for leaving France and called for war with Europe. Lafayette's zenith had passed—he had lost an election for mayor of Paris in November and had left the National Guard for his rural home. "[H]is Sun seems to be totally set," Morris wrote to Robert Morris, "unless he should put himself at the head of the republican Party [the Girondins] who at present are much opposed to him. All this," he added frankly, "results from Feebleness of Character and the Spirit of Intrigue, which bring forward the Courtier but ruin the Statesman."

The harvest of 1791 was poor, leading to price increases and the first stirrings on the streets of the future instrument of the

Terror, the men who called themselves *sans-culottes*. Morris urged Montmorin to make arrangements to distribute food in the king's name. Montmorin, whose political influence was waning, did not pursue the notion and admitted what Morris already knew, that he had "not Force enough of Character to pursue the Measures which he knows to be right." Morris wrote directly to the king on the subject, and sent a copy of his letter to Montmorin to the queen at her request; but to no avail.

The Girondins were not alone in calling for war in the fall of 1791. Louis hoped that war would be, as Morris had previously suggested, the "great friend to Sovereign Authority." His wife, by contrast, hoped that the French armies would be defeated by the Austrians and Prussians, who would put Louis back in power. Her secret efforts in this regard did not prevent her from continuing to solicit Morris's advice.

The more radical Jacobin Club, however, was divided on the issue of war. The club, which had once been an association of moderate reformers, now included men such as Danton and Robespierre, the future icons of the most violent periods of the Revolution. Robespierre worried that the country was unprepared for war, and Morris, who no longer supported war, was of the same opinion. He thought the king would be better off working to maintain the peace, "leaving the Assembly to act as they may think proper," which would have destructive results that would "demonstrate the necessity of restoring in a great degree the royal authority." He despised the émigrés and those still in Louis's court "burning with the lust of vengeance, most of them poor, and all of them proud," who hoped through a war to "re-establish that species of despotism most suited to their own cupidity."

Morris's opinion of the French military situation was not improved by Louis's appointment of Madame de Staël's longtime lover (and Talleyrand's friend) the unimpressive Comte de Narbonne as minister of war, and an ineffective man named Delessart to foreign affairs. The two men came from different court factions: Narbonne and the minister of the marine Bernard de Moleville (who would become a good friend of Morris) considered themselves moderates who continued to advocate the "principles" of the early days of the Revolution. Delessart and Duport, the king's keeper of the seals, belonged to a more radical faction, though the Champs de Mars massacre had toned them down considerably. There was tension between these groups, and the new ministry was "strongly opposed by the Assembly," according to Morris. Nonetheless, they pushed for war, and at the end of December Lafayette was given command of one of France's armies.

War with the Austrians and Prussians made a neutral England desirable, and Talleyrand, who had abandoned his bishopric to become an administrator in Paris, was sent to London to seek British neutrality. "This is a most wretched Policy," Morris wrote, believing the neutrality request would benefit only England. Morris was on his way to London on business himself, leaving on January 22, 1792, and before he left Viq d'Azyr, the queen's counselor, told him the queen had asked to be told of anything "in England interesting to them," a remarkable indication of the interest the royal family took in Morris. While he was away, he would learn of his appointment as the new American minister plenipotentiary to France.

Washington's choice of Morris proved controversial for a number of reasons. Morris was already disliked by many in America for his activities during the American Revolution—as a French consul in America put it, the Americans "admire but fear his genius."

His opponents felt vindicated in their poor opinion of him by the spread of Hamilton's fabrications about his mission to London. Washington himself believed that the British disliked him, which was why he named Morris to Paris instead of London. According to the editors of his papers, Jefferson opposed sending Morris to Paris, for he was increasingly disturbed by the reports from France—particularly from William Short, who was hell-bent on getting the position himself—that Morris was detested by the French.

Washington's support was enough, barely enough, to get Morris's nomination confirmed. James Monroe—who would be Morris's successor in 1794—particularly objected: "His manners are not conciliatory—his character well known [and] considered as indiscreet. . . . Besides he is a monarchy man [and] not suitable to be employed by this country, nor in France. He went to Europe to sell lands and Certificates."

Aaron Burr denounced him as well. Roger Sherman, whom Morris had admired during the Constitutional Convention, called Morris "an irreligious and profane man—he is no hypocrite and never pretended to have any religion." Sherman compared him to Benedict Arnold, and said the nation should not give positions of trust to such men, a remark that would have shocked Morris if he had heard it.

Washington also named Thomas Pinckney to London, and William Short to the Hague to handle the remaining debt payment issues. The vote, taken on January 12, 1792, demonstrated the extent of Morris's unpopularity and the limits of Washington's prestige: Morris was confirmed by a 16 to 11 vote; Thomas Pinckney was confirmed for London with no dissents. Monroe wrote to a friend that the opposition to Morris was founded in his general moral character wh[ich] precluded all possibility of confidence in his morals. 2ndly his known attachment to monarchic govt. & contempt of the Republicans, rendering him unfit to represent us & especially at the French court in the present happy turn of their affairs. 3d. his general brutality of manners & indiscretion giving him a wonderful facility in making enemies & losing friends & of course unfit for a negotiator—4thly his being at present abroad as a vendor of public securities & back lands.

Jefferson was by this time equally negative about Morris. A month after the appointment, Washington refused to write a letter of congratulation to the French regarding their new constitution, telling Jefferson he did not know that the king "in his heart approved" the constitution, and that he had begun to "doubt very much the affairs of France." Jefferson, who exulted in the constitution, immediately blamed Morris. In his private notes of the meeting he wrote: "The fact is that Gouverneur Morris, a high flying Monarchy-man, shutting his eyes and his faith to every fact against his wishes, and believing every thing he desires to be true, has kept the President's mind constantly poisoned with his forebodings."

Few today question that the record demonstrates that it was *Jefferson* who resolutely closed "his eyes and his faith to every fact against his wishes" regarding the French Revolution. Yet Jefferson's antagonism toward Morris did not simply derive from a genuine difference of views on France; it was fueled regularly by reports to Jefferson from a phalanx of people hostile to Morris for their own reasons. William Short was the most prolific source of angry complaints, for Morris stood in the way of Short's heart's desire. Ever since Jefferson's departure from Paris he had kept up a continual stream of letters (better described as demands) that Jefferson obtain the position of minister for him, though Jefferson told him flatly he could not, and in fact did not consider Short an appropriate choice. As soon as he realized that Morris was a possible contender, Short—who professed friendship to Morris himself—began to denounce him to Jefferson, and Jefferson apparently believed a fair amount of it. It was shabby. Morris helped Short in many ways, repeatedly defending him against the criticisms of the French who found the fussy and occasionally abrasive young man irritating. Morris once even snapped at the lovely wife of the British ambassador, a particular friend of his, when she attacked Short in conversation. He even helped protect the property of Short's lover, Rosalie de Rochefoucauld, while she and her family were in prison during the Terror, and did all he could to get news about her to Short.

Short was not Morris's only enemy. Thomas Paine had long disliked Morris, though he pretended otherwise, visiting him regularly in London and Paris and frequently borrowing money. He, too, promptly wrote to Jefferson denouncing the appointment. William Stephens Smith, Hamilton's unofficial envoy to London, did not have anything against Morris personally, but resented him for having obtained the nomination. Smith also saw him as an annoying obstacle to various business schemes, including the sale of military supplies to a proposed French expedition against Spain in Venezuela. William Jackson, the dilatory secretary of the Constitutional Convention, who later came to France on business, did not like Morris either, and did his best to damage him with the French government. All the negative reports of these men, made to Jefferson and others, could not help but have a cumulative damaging effect on the perception of Morris.

Morris heard of his nomination while he was preparing to leave Europe. He was worried about the deterioration of Robert Morris's business affairs, and Morrisania had been too long without its owner in residence. He was apparently struck speechless—his diary entry for the day states only that he had heard the news from William Constable. He did not hear for another six weeks that he had been confirmed, and it must have been an uncomfortable period, for the reports from the United States made it clear that the nomination was hanging "by the eyelids."

Morris was not eager to accept the assignment, writing to Robert that if he were to consult "only my own Feelings and my own Interest I should certainly not accept it." He knew all too well that "[t]he mission to France must be a stormy one, let if fall on whom it may," because "[t]o stand *well* with all Parties is impossible." And he was wounded at the news of the bitter opposition to his appointment. Nonetheless, Morris felt duty-bound to accept the post, and when it was confirmed he threw himself into the preparations, taking advantage of being in London to procure his "outfit," for which he was allotted a full year's salary. He bought horses, new dishes, malmsey and Madeira, a coach, and books, and he began to look for a secretary.

The vitriol against Morris in America was matched in France. Brissot de Warville's paper *Le Patriote Français* published an insulting letter about the appointment, possibly written by Thomas Paine. James Swan, who planned to exploit his association with Morris in his own business ventures, worried that Brissot's animosity might interfere, and went to talk to him. He reported to Morris that Brissot said

> he was sure of the facts, & knew your intimacy with the Royal party, & your sentiments on the Constitution. I mention'd many faults in that [the constitution] which were too striking not to meet his ideas, & were too great not to receive the disapproba-

tion of you & every sensible person. He concluded that he who was friend to the aristocrates, or were intimate with the present [illegible] of the executive, must be enemies to the opinions of the majority of the people . . . & therefore the greatest part of the nation could have no confidance in you.

Swan told Morris that he suspected that Brissot's "uncommon rancour against you" was "fed by some interest concealed"—specifically, a fear that Morris would interfere with Brissot's continuing hope of taking over the balance of the U.S. debt to France. He was very likely right, but whatever Brissot's true motives, Morris's effectiveness as minister would be sorely damaged by the Girondin leader's repeated public attacks.

CHAPTER ELEVEN

THE KING FALLS

GOUVERNEUR MORRIS WOULD SPEND MUCH OF HIS FIRST FEW months as American minister to France trying to help Louis XVI escape. Theodore Roosevelt later concluded that Morris thereby put his country's interests at risk. But he found it "impossible to blame" him, because Morris was convinced that "his own exertions were all that lay between the two unfortunate sovereigns and their fate," which "roused his gallantry and blinded him to the risk." Indeed, Morris grieved as he saw the Revolution descend into violent anarchy.

Despite continuing hostility from successive French governments, Morris remained in France through the Terror and did his best to protect Americans and American interests. It was a Herculean labor. During his twenty-nine months as minister (April 1792–July 1794), there would be eight different representatives of foreign affairs, which reflected a series of usually bloody shifts of power. Six of the men he dealt with under the different regimes would be condemned by the successor government as traitors; of these six, one was murdered by a mob, one was guillotined, one was imprisoned, and one escaped to Austria.

Perhaps it would be appropriate to pause here in order to examine Morris's particular hopes for the outcome of the French Revolution. They bear repeating in the face of two hundred years of insistent and unsophisticated charges that he was, as Jefferson put it, a "high-flying Monarchy man." Morris had seen and heard enough of the ancien régime to abhor it, and he repeatedly expressed the wish that France could be the means of extending reform and freedom throughout Europe. He hoped that if King Louis could escape Paris, he might yet establish a constitutional, limited monarchy. Believing that the situation was already one of virtual anarchy, he feared that the door was now open to absolutism, thanks to the poor judgment of men such as Lafayette, men whom he termed the "inconsiderate Partizans of Liberty." He told Jefferson that he feared that the threat of foreign invasion might drive the French—as it eventually did—to embrace "Despotism as a Blessing, if accompanied with Security to Person and Property, such as is experienced under the worst Governments of Europe."

While still in London, he sent letters of advice to a former *département* administrator named Terrier du Monciel, who, at Morris's recommendation to Louis, had obtained a position as one of the inner circle of royal counselors. Morris's judgment of Monciel would prove well founded, for Monciel worked for the king to the bitter end. The French ministry had been shuffled yet again, prompting Morris to remark to Short that "the Ministerial Seats resemble electrical Chairs which give every Occupant a kick in the Breeches." Narbonne and Moleville had become openly hostile over the question of war, and the king dismissed Narbonne. The Girondins were furious and pushed through an indictment of the weak foreign minister Delessart for treason; Brissot admitted privately that the allegations were fabricated, but he wanted him out of the ministry. Delessart was imprisoned at Versailles and would be murdered there in the September 1792 massacres, prompting one acute political observer to comment that "Brissot was faithful to his party, but a traitor to integrity." These events were enough to convince Moleville that he should resign his official post, although he continued to serve as a close counselor to the king.

The successor ministry was the first Girondin ministry, the result of the influence of Charles-François Dumouriez, a veteran soldier who was playing a dangerous game of cultivating both the court and the Girondins. He was appointed to foreign affairs and, at his instigation and as a concession to the Girondins, Roland de la Platière (and thereby his famously powerful wife, Marie-Jeanne Roland de la Platière) was chosen for the interior and Etienne Clavière—the erstwhile Swiss speculator in the American debt— was made head of finances. The new minister of war, Pierre de Grave, whom Morris thought fatally weak, would soon be replaced (at Mme. Roland de la Platière's behest) with the fiery Joseph Servan. The result was a cabinet filled with tension and very different objectives, some of them secret.

On April 20, 1792, France declared war on Austria, marking the beginning of decades of war in Europe. The first few months went badly for the French: their initial plan of taking Flanders in a cakewalk floundered when the Flemish declined to rise against the Austrians. The French troops were ill-trained and insubordinate, with dangerous tensions between the rank-and-file and the officers, many of whom were former nobles. One of the generals was assassinated by his men after a defeat, leading some officers, including the famous Rochambeau, to resign. "[T]he Troops are every where in Mutiny and La Fayette's Army without Necessaries of every Kind," Morris wrote in mid-May. "The Horses dead, the Soldiers sick and weary, and the Officers apprehensive and discontented."

Morris had returned to Paris from England on May 6, 1792. He found an official residence on the Rue de la Planche, on the Left Bank, and set about having it furnished and decorated, but he was disconcerted to hear from Adèle that Dumouriez would refuse to receive his credentials. James Swan told Morris that Short was behind the planned rebuff; Morris refused to believe it, but it may well have been true, for Short, who was behaving boorishly in his disappointment, was hopeful that the French would reject Morris and leave Short in place as *chargé*. However, on May 15, with bad grace, he presented Morris to Dumouriez: "The Interview here is very short," wrote Morris.

> I tell him that I have a small favor to ask of the King, which is that he will receive me without a Sword because of my wooden Leg. He says there will be no Difficulty as to that Matter and adds that I am already acquainted with the King. I reply that I never saw his Majesty but in public nor ever exchanged a Word with him in my life, altho some of their Gazettes have made of me one of his Ministers; and that I am perswaded he would not know me if he should see me.

There then followed a remarkable exchange between these two men, each of whom was presenting a false front—Dumouriez, by appearing to be a follower of the Girondins, and Morris, who knew Dumouriez's game, by claiming to have detached himself from French politics. Dumouriez commented that people believed Morris to be close to the king. Morris responded:

> I am naturally frank and open and therefore do not hesitate to say that in the Time of the Constituent Assembly I endeavor'd, being then a private Individual and prompted by my Regard for this Nation, to effect certain Changes in the Constitution which appear'd to me essential to its' Existence. That I was not successful, and being at present a public man I consider it as my Duty not to meddle with their Affairs.

His report of the meeting to Jefferson said nearly the same thing, and Morris described himself as a "meer Spectator."

This declaration by Morris—first to the foreign minister of France and then to his own secretary of state—is incredible, in view of his continuing activities on behalf of the king. It is true that meaningful discussion of his actions with his own government was impossible. He knew that his letters were often opened and read (contrary to international law). To send a request for instructions and receive a response could take as long as six months, which would make the instructions virtually meaningless in the rapid change of events. In any event, his involvement in French politics continued unabated: he continued to consult regularly with his "moles"—including Brémond—and with the inner counselors of the king, including Montmorin and Moleville.

The early military setbacks raised the fear that enemy troops would invade Paris by mid-June. Widespread anxiety was exacerbated by a fear of famine, and there were sporadic riots throughout the country and violent demands for price controls and sanctions against alleged hoarders of food supplies. "The Dilapidation in every Department is unexampled," Morris wrote to Jefferson, and the military and political situations were in total disarray. The nationalized church land "is consumed and the Debt is as great as at the Opening of the States General." The "best Picture I can give of the French nation is that of Cattle before a Thunder Storm," Morris told the secretary of state, and "every Member of [the Government] is engaged in the Defense of himself or the Attack of his Neighbor." Because of the constant shifting of the people in power, Jefferson's instructions to pursue commercial advantages for the United States were impossible to fulfill—cultivating anyone in government who might be thrown out the next month could mean the next dealings would be with "[p]ersons who would oppose a Measure merely because their Predecessors have approved of it."

Morris continued to hope that the military and economic situations would cause the French people to place their faith in the king, but he was dismayed by the king's indecisiveness. It was a shortcoming that the king's most loyal friend, Malesherbes, described as "excessive timidity." Morris, who met Louis face-to-face for the first time when he presented his credentials at court on June 3, called it "feebleness." Morris was wrong in this assessment: Louis was not a coward, and Morris would later record his admiration for the king's "uncommon firmness in suffering." Nonetheless, the hope that King Louis could take command was doomed by the Girondins' unceasing effort to paint the court as treasonously conspiring with the Austrians and Prussians (as Marie Antoinette was in fact doing). At the same time, the Girondin-led Assembly passed measures to further diminish Louis's power.

In early June, a decree was passed to call up twenty thousand soldiers, the *fédérés,* from all over France to come to Paris as a quasi-army that would frustrate any efforts by the king to leave. The people's suspicions of Louis were increased when he refused to sanction this decree, along with another that required those priests who refused to swear obedience to the Civil Constitution to be deported. When Servan, Clavière, and Roland objected to his vetoes, Louis dismissed them, and the Girondins denounced the court. Monciel was named to replace Roland as minister of the interior. Fearful of an outright breach with the Assembly, Dumouriez tried to convince the king to retract his vetoes. When he refused, Dumouriez resigned and left to take command of the Army of the North.

On June 17, Morris wrote to Jefferson that the Jacobins had gone to the Assembly with a petition to suspend the king. "[W]e stand on a vast Volcano," he wrote. "We feel it tremble and we hear it roar but how and when and where it will burst and who may be destroy'd by its Eruptions is beyond the Ken of mortal Foresight to discover." He reported that Lafayette was planning to bring troops to Paris to oust the radicals, and that he was "not sanguine as to the Success. Very much is to be done and there is very little Time to do it, for the foreign enemy will soon be greatly superior in Number." The country's political situation was dire:

> [W]hile a great Part of the Nation is desirous of overturning the present Government in order to restore the antient Form, and while another Part still more dangerous from Position and Numbers are desirous of introducing the Form of a federal Republic, the moderate Men, attack'd on all Sides, have to contend alone against an immense Force. I cannot go on with the Picture for my Heart bleeds when I reflect that the finest Opportunity which ever presented itself for establishing the Rights of Mankind throughout the civilized World is perhaps lost and forever.

Lafayette did not march on Paris, but he did publish a letter excoriating the Jacobins. While some in the Assembly applauded, others branded Lafayette a traitor, and the former idol of the Revolution was denounced throughout Paris. On June 20, a crowd of radical members of the Paris Sections occupied the Tuileries Palace and cornered the king. For four long hours, Louis's biographer writes, the king "stood on a window seat with nothing between him and the mob but a table and a handful of grenadiers"; among those "grenadiers" was his new minister of the interior, Terrier du Monciel. At the mob's insistence, Louis put on a Phrygian cap, the symbol of the common man, and raised a glass to *la nation,* but he still refused to sanction the decree against the priests and the decree calling up the *fédérés.*

The invasion of the Tuileries was a profound shock to many, including Morris, who at last recognized the great danger to the king. "The Constitution has this Day I think given its last Groan," he wrote. He recommended to Monciel that Mayor Pétion of Paris, who had deliberately done nothing to prevent the Tuileries assault, be suspended and the other ringleaders prosecuted. Mayor Pétion was suspended, but he would be restored within weeks, and on June 25 Morris heard of another plot to break into the Tuileries. For the moment, this plan was discarded. On the 28th, Lafayette came to the Assembly without his troops, spoke against the Jacobins and against the events of June 20, and attempted without success to unite the National Guard behind him.

Morris saw the former marquis the next day while at court, and Lafayette spoke to him in "the Ton[e] of ancient Familiarity," probably in melancholy acknowledgment that Morris's long-expressed fears about the Revolution had come to pass. Morris urged Lafayette to return to his army immediately, lest he be imprisoned as a traitor. He must, Morris told him, "determine to fight for a good Constitution or for that wretched Piece of Paper which bears the Name, or in six weeks"—Morris had it down to the very day—"it will be too late." Lafayette's response, as always, was disappointing, and the conversation petered out. Morris would not see Lafayette again for more than five years.

From this time on, Morris was determined to help salvage the situation. He began sending advice to the king through Monciel, for the only means of establishing a new and functional constitution would be, he still believed, through the king. There had been a swell of loyal indignation in the nation's regional *départements* against the events of June 20. Morris and Monciel hoped that this might provide the impetus to restore the king's influence and destroy that of the Assembly. Monciel ordered the *départements* to block the *fédérés* from marching to Paris, and he had a denunciation of June 20 circulated within the armies and throughout the country.

Morris and Monciel had some success. In Paris, thousands signed a petition denouncing the events of June 20. This alarmed the Girondins, and on July 2 Monciel was summoned to the Assembly and denounced as a traitor amid the deafening shouts of the members. The scene must have been terrifying. Monciel was blocked from leaving until a guard came to clear his path. When he saw Morris later that day, Monciel told him frankly that the French were "too rotten for a free government." They must have concluded that Louis had no alternative but to escape Paris, and they began to work with others who believed likewise.

Several escape plans were discussed during the summer of 1792, and it is difficult now to sort out the precise sequence of events. Morris's diary entries are occasionally inconsistent with a memorandum he wrote a few years later, and other somewhat inconsistent accounts were written by others, including Moleville, Malouet (a well-known moderate), and Lafayette. It appears, however, that there were essentially three major escape efforts, the last occurring only a few days before the fall of the monarchy. Each time, the conspirators would run into the obduracy of the king, which was due in large measure to the queen, who was in contact with foreign courts and hoped for an invasion that would forcibly return her husband to power. Montmorin, who had been involved with the flight to Varennes, was involved with the queen's subplots, probably more than Morris knew, and although he was present at many of the discussions of escape, he generally opposed it.

The group also included the Comte de Clermont-Tonnerre, who had helped orchestrate the merging of the three Estates in 1789. Morris was apparently the most energetic member; Malouet later wrote that Morris "gave His Majesty, although more fruitlessly than we did, much more vigorous advice." They seem not to have dwelled on the fact that they had different objectives. Lafayette wanted to work within the framework of the existing constitution; Malouet and Morris hoped for a constitutional monarchy under a better constitution; and Moleville dreamed of a return to the ancien régime. The king and queen also had different goals. The king hoped for a good constitution; the queen wanted a return to an absolute monarchy, and she believed this could be achieved only by foreign intervention. She repeatedly implored Austria and Prussia to publish a formal threat of invasion (the so-called Brunswick Manifesto), with the fatal miscalculation that the frightened populace would turn to Louis to save them. Morris, on the other hand, believed that the foreign powers would partition France and squelch all reform. It is clear that although Marie Antoinette asked

Morris's advice numerous times that summer, he was unaware of her intentions and that she was supplying intelligence to the Austrians and Prussians.

The first escape plan had already been sketched out before Morris joined the group in late June. On July 15 Lafayette and loyal members of the National Guard, as well as the king's personal Swiss bodyguards, would escort Louis to the royal palace at Compiègne. The king would then issue a public declaration forbidding his brothers and the other foreign forces from invading France. (Louis's brothers—the comte de Provence and future Louis XVIII, and the comte d'Artois—had left France in 1789 and had been plotting a counterrevolutionary offensive ever since.)

While Morris, Monciel, and the others worked to get Louis's agreement and hammered out the logistics, the level of rhetoric against the monarchy crossed the same threshold that the invaders of the Tuileries had crossed weeks before. In the Assembly, one member claimed that Lafayette's visit to Paris on June 28 had constituted treason because he had left his troops to make the trip. This member demanded that Lafayette be imprisoned and sent to Orléans. Another member accused Louis of deliberately seeking the military's defeat. The Assembly defied Louis's refusal to sanction the *fédérés* and invited them to Paris for the Bastille celebrations on July 14.

In Morris's view,

> [t]hings are now verging fast to the Catastrophe of the Play. For some Weeks the adverse Parties, I mean the Court and [J]acobines, have been laboring each to cast on the other the odium of violating entirely the Constitution, and commencing the civil War. The Party which calls itself independent, and which in Fact is the fearful Party, begs hard for Peace, and seizes eagerly whatever bears the Appearance of the Name.

The king was due to make a decision about the escape on July 10, but the day passed and nothing happened. The next morning Morris was informed that "their Majesties flash'd in the Pan." Marie Antoinette had turned the plan down because of her distrust of Lafayette and because her foreign advisors had recommended staying in Paris.

The king's refusal to act meant his ministers were put in great danger of discovery for their efforts. The ministers of foreign affairs, the navy, finance, and justice all resigned, though they continued in an acting capacity for a while. In late July, having heard rumors that he was to be formally accused of treason, Monciel was allowed to resign but continued in the circle of inner counselors, visiting Montmorin regularly and talking to the king in the evenings.

In the meantime, Morris, Monciel, Moleville, and others began taking steps to protect Louis should an insurrection begin. Among these efforts was raising what Morris described later as a "sort of royal army." They designated agents in the National Guard, who gathered intelligence and recruited others who would, supposedly, stand by the king. These actions required money, so Moleville obtained donations totaling around 2.5 million livres. In late July, the king asked Morris, through Monciel, to "become guardian of his papers and his money," adding that Morris had "always given him good Advice and he has the greatest Confidence in me." Morris reluctantly agreed. The money was promptly put into service to distribute to "counter-conspirators."

Morris was not optimistic about the success of these plans, and on July 17 he told Montmorin that King Louis should leave Paris. Like Marie Antoinette, Montmorin was placing his hopes in the foreign allies, indulging, in Morris's words, in "a thousand empty Hopes and vain Expectations."

The situation was growing rapidly more dangerous. On the evening of July 25, Santerre, head of the National Guard of a radical Parisian *faubourg* (political district), and Westermann, a leader of the *fédérés,* planned an attack on the Tuileries. But when the tocsin was rung in the middle of the night to summon the attackers, it went unanswered.

The Girondins belatedly began to realize that their unceasing attacks on the king's authority, intended to give them the ability to control the crown and the nation, had pushed France to the point of a complete overthrow of the monarchy. In a desperate effort to undo what could not be undone, they offered Louis a deal: he could continue as king in exchange for reappointing the three Girondin ministers he had dismissed in the spring. Louis rebuffed them. Moleville would later claim that the Girondins were actually pursuing what amounted to protection money.

The latest escape plan had not been abandoned, though the king still had not agreed to it. Morris and Monciel arranged for a message to go to Lafayette, presumably to call him to help protect the king in a retreat; but some of these plans must have been leaked. Brissot told the Assembly that Lafayette was planning to march on Paris. "I verily believe that if Mr. de La Fayette were to appear just now in Paris unattended by his Army he would be torn to Pieces," Morris wrote Secretary of State Jefferson on August 1. Morris told him that there were "Plans in Agitation at present to establish a good Constitution," but declined to provide details because "should my Letter miscarry it would occasion much of that Noise and Nonsense in which it is unpleasant to find one's Name. And the wrongheaded People who get hold of such Things cannot distinguish between a Person who has obtain'd exact Information of what is doing and those who are Actors in the Business."

Morris *was* an actor "in the Business," but he was right that it would have been extremely dangerous not only to himself but to others if he had told Jefferson what was actually taking place; he may also have hoped that this letter would protect the United States from French suspicion if he were caught.

The conspirators now apparently agreed on a modified plan. The royal family would go to a location in Normandy, thirty-six miles from the coast, allowing them to leave the country if it became necessary. The king's master of the Civil List (the king's private funds), Arnaud De La Porte, would invite Montmorin and Clermont-Tonnerre to dinner, and they would hide the family in their coaches and drive out of the city while fifty Swiss Guards kept the barrier sentinels occupied. Fifteen hundred Swiss Guards would go from their current station at Courbevoie to protect the escape route. Once established in Normandy, King Louis would publish an address explaining his actions to the French people. Morris wrote Jefferson that he could feel no more than a wish that Louis would succeed. Real hope was not possible, because "I have no Confidence in the Morals of the People. The King is anxious to secure their permanent Happiness but Alas they are not in a State of Mind to receive Good from his Hands. Suspicion, that constant Companion of Vice and Weakness, has loosened every Band of social Union and blasts every honest Hope in the Moment of its budding."

The Brunswick Manifesto was published on August 3. It informed the French that the Prussians would punish them if they harmed the royal family or attempted to resist the Prussian and Austrian armies. Morris had already predicted its destructive effect. He described it disdainfully as saying "Be all against me, for I am opposed to you all; and make a good resistance, for there is no longer any hope." The reaction against the king, who was assumed to have solicited the proclamation (as Queen Marie Antoinette had actually done) was fierce. Forty-seven of the forty-eight sections of Paris sent a petition to the Assembly denouncing the king, and plans began for an attack by the *fédérés*. The loyal group of counselors met on August 4 and made one last effort to finalize a new escape plan. When Montmorin visited the king that evening, he apparently agreed to cooperate.

When Morris returned home from the meeting, he found his friend Lady Sutherland, the wife of the British ambassador, waiting for him. She and her husband were undoubtedly aware of the plan and may have participated, for she had come to Morris to ask him to speak to the Chevalier de Coigny, who wished to give Morris's "ideas direct to the queen without passing thro the Medium of Monsieur de Montmorin." The reason for the queen's request was clear: "They all expect to be murdered this Evening at the Chateau."

When Morris and Monciel met with Coigny on August 6, they apparently agreed on a speech for the king to deliver to the *fédérés* that would be welcomed by paid agents who had infiltrated their ranks. Meanwhile, Moleville sent word to Louis to plan on departing that night or the next. The long day passed with no response until, at six o'clock, Moleville learned that the king had directed suspension of all "preparations for their departure until farther notice; as it was their majesties' intentions to reserve that step for the last extremity." Moleville later recalled: "These fatal words were like a thunderbolt to me. 'What do they mean by the last extremity?' cried I, with as much rage as despair. 'Who can the idiots or traitors be, who have suggested such a pernicious resolution?'"

Moleville later learned that the queen opposed going to Normandy. Given the reliable intelligence of an imminent attack,

Moleville was beside himself. He hurried to Montmorin's to entreat him to try and change the king's mind. Montmorin agreed to write to the king, but he also said,

> I am sure that they are swayed by different counsel than ours. The king is ruined, my friend, and so are we all. You laughed at me six months ago, when I told you it would come to a republic: you will find that I was not deceived; I believe it is at no great distance; perhaps it will not last long; but that will depend upon the fate of the king. If he is assassinated, the republic will certainly be of short duration; but if he shall be formally tried, and consequently condemned, you will not have the monarchy so soon re-established.

Less than four weeks later, Montmorin would lie dead on the stones of the courtyard of the Abbaye Prison.

The following day, Morris's group agreed to a new plan to bring the king out under the protection of loyal National Guardsmen, who would rendezvous with Swiss Guards and escort the family out of Paris. When there was no answer to his note, Montmorin went to talk to the king. The king's sister told him "that the insurrection was not really close at hand; that Santerre and Pétion had promised, and that they had received 750,000 livres to bring the Marseillais over to his Majesty's side. The King was no longer uneasy, but determined not to leave Paris." Despite Louis's rejection of the plan, someone must have sent orders to the Swiss Guards, for on August 9, between two and three o'clock in the morning, two battalions of Swiss Guards left their posts for the palace in Paris.

It is possible that Morris was behind the efforts to bribe Santerre and Mayor Pétion; as noted earlier, he was involved in some such effort to infiltrate and manipulate the *fédérés,* using the king's money; and it is well known that Marie Antoinette was determined not to leave Paris. However, Morris's papers clearly indicate that after the invasion of the Tuileries in late June he was a firm advocate of the king's escape, and that his efforts to bribe the *fédérés* were only contingency plans should escape fail and an insurrection begin in Paris. In any case, Malouet, who may not have known about Morris's activities, later denounced this "miserable intrigue" with the most "furious Jacobins," because he believed it gave the royal family false hopes of a successful counterrevolution.

The group met again on the night of August 7, after the king had rejected the last plan of escape. They discussed the possibility of having Louis step down and instituting a regency, but it seemed unworkable. Finally, distraught, they went home. They would not meet again.

On the hot morning of Thursday, August 9, Monciel brought Morris more money from Louis; the sum of two hundred thousand livres appears the following day in Morris's statement of accounts. Morris dressed and went to court for what would be the last time, visited Adèle, and had dinner with the British ambassador and his wife. "Afterwards call at Mon. Montmorin's and go thence to Madame d'Albani's, where I stay till near twelve. Paris is in great Agitation."

The following morning, the waiting ended. At 7:30, Roederer, another of the king's advisors, came to the Tuileries Palace to tell Louis and a disbelieving Marie Antoinette they must leave the palace and go to the Assembly to take refuge. A few hours later, "the Cannon begin, and Musquetry mingled with them announce a warm Day," Morris wrote in his home across the Seine. A flood of angry people engulfed the palace while the hope of a counterrevolutionary force melted in the air. Only the Swiss Guards and Louis's few personal friends—including Montmorin and the elderly Malesherbes—fought the invaders. The National Guardsmen who had been assigned to protect the palace broke their swords and fled. Urged on by the *fédéré* Westermann, who would be named a general as a reward for his work, the crowds swept through, slaughtering all who resisted. The hunt soon spread to the streets, and Morris's fellow conspirators were among the targets. Their agent in the National Guard was caught; he would lose his head less than two weeks later, followed by De La Porte. Clermont-Tonnerre was hunted down and beaten to death. Montmorin hid in the home of a laundress but was found and dragged to prison. Others, including Malouet, managed to evade the search and would eventually escape France. A number of people hurried to Morris's legation to take refuge, including Adèle and her son. The next day Morris wrote: "A sleepless Night renders me heavy during this Day. The King & Queen remain yet at the Assembly which goes on rapidly under the *Dictée* of the Tribunes. We are quiet here. Things are taking on their new Order. The Weather continues to be very hot. Mr. de St. Pardou calls in the Evening and seems to be torn to pieces by Affliction. I desire him, if he sees the royal Family, to tell them that Relief must soon arrive." But it was a false hope Morris offered. The "Relief" was presumably Lafayette, but Lafayette's troops ignored his efforts to rally them. The man who had three years before been the darling of France would shortly be condemned as a traitor and forced to flee.

In the early morning of August 12, Monciel and his wife came to Morris for safety. "The Weather is very warm still and even oppressive," Morris wrote. "The State of the Air is evidenced by some Perch which, alive in the Morning at six oClock are spoil'd at Dinner. So rapid a State of putrefaction I never yet saw."

Over the next few days many others must have come to the legation, for when a young American named Thomas Griffith went to see Morris that week, he found "a number of gentlemen and ladies" who, Morris told him, "from former intercourse with America, and in many cases services rendered to the United States, considered themselves entitled to protection in the hotel of the minister." He told Griffith, "I did not invite them to come, but . . . I will not put them out now that they are here, let the consequences be what they may."

Six days after the attack on the Tuileries, and only seven days after he last saw King Louis at court, Morris wrote Jefferson: "Another Revolution has been effected in this City. It was bloody." Since only Lafayette had any military force, he expected that the last chance to change the situation "will be suffered to pass away. I have long been convinced that this middle party, who by the bye were the prime movers of the revolution, must fall to the Ground." Morris had indeed predicted the failure of Lafayette and his circle from the beginning, though he had desperately tried to avert it. But he found no satisfaction in having been proven right.

On August 13, he wrote to Thomas Pinckney in London: "An American has a stronger Sympathy with this Country than any other Observer and nourished as he is in the very Bosom of Liberty he cannot but be deeply afflicted to see that in almost every Event this Struggle must terminate in Despotism. Yet such is the melancholy Spectacle which presents itself to my Mind and with which it has long been occupied." It was, he noted, a "painful reflection that one of the first countries in the world should be so cruelly torn to pieces." He knew that the violence had barely begun:

> The Storm which lately raged is a little subsided but the Winds must soon rise again perhaps from the same perhaps from anoth-

er Quarter but that is of little Consequence since in every Case we must expect a like Rape and Devastation. A Man attached to his fellow Men must see with the same Distress the Woes they suffer whether arising from an Army or from a Mob and whether those by whom they were inflicted speak [F]rench or [G]erman.

Thomas Jefferson and others in America who, as Morris once commented, designed governments "in their Closets" based on "Men as exist nowhere and least of all in France," could not begin to comprehend the spectacle of an ancient society now imploding with such violence. Morris would remain in France for the next two years and witness the bloody fulfillment of his fears; it is a testimony to his understanding of human nature that the horrors he saw would neither surprise him nor diminish his capacity for compassion.

Whether Morris exhibited good judgment in attempting to help King Louis is an open question. Morris would probably have defended his efforts on the grounds that he and the others who still hoped to salvage a constitutional monarchy had no alternative—because both the Girondins and the monarchs gave them none. Another debatable question is whether Morris, whatever his hopes for France, should have done these things when occupying the post of minister to France. It seems likely that, as a representative of a new republic that owed its existence to the French, Morris felt that he must do what he could to help the French achieve the government with the "greatest degree of liberty that the people could bear," as Jefferson had put it—and the king, however inept, was the only available instrument for this end. Morris, for his part, had no regrets; in July 1792, while planning to help the king escape Paris, Morris wrote to his brother-in-law in which he challenged "the World to produce against me a single Instance of mean or cruel or dishonest or dishonorable Conduct." With respect to his actions during the Revolution, this is not a challenge that is easily met.

CHAPTER TWELVE

INTO THE TERROR

THE FALL OF LOUIS XVI TRANSFORMED THE NATURE OF Gouverneur Morris's duties as minister to France. Instead of working to advance French-American commerce—the principal theme of Secretary of State Thomas Jefferson's first instructions to him—he began protecting Americans engaged in that commerce from the inevitable disruptions and losses caused by the spreading European war. He did so in isolation—all the other ministers left after August 10, 1792. He also did so in the face of a series of hostile revolutionary governments, for though each successor regime to Louis XVI denounced its predecessor, they were all in agreement in their vilification of the monarchy, which by definition meant that they distrusted Morris, who, they knew, had tried to save it. They did not care about the niceties of his pursuit of a limited constitutional monarchy. He was seen as a monarchist and that was enough. Their efforts to have him recalled began almost immediately.

It is interesting to speculate about whether Morris continued to be involved in secret projects on behalf of the deposed monarch while he was still in France. Unfortunately, his papers say nothing about any such activity after August 1792. In a diary entry dated January 5, 1793, he wrote: "The Situation of Things is such that to continue this Journal would compromise many People. . . . I prefer therefore the more simple Measure of putting an End to it." Who would have been compromised and for what activities is unknown. He did not begin the diary again until he was leaving France for good.

Morris would find working as a minister under the new order supremely thankless. His countrymen who were in France believed that he was not aggressive enough in his demands for restitution (many ships and crews had been seized by French privateers) or in his actions on behalf of hapless American citizens thrown into jail with other suspect foreigners. French officials believed the opposite, for they resented any petition, however moderately presented, that by its very nature illustrated their failure to honor French obligations to neutral shipping or the arbitrariness of the system that threw thousands of innocent people into jail.

Morris did not share the outrage of many former Francophiles in America over French depredations on American ships or the arrests of Americans, though he worked ceaselessly for redress. He was too aware of the desperate situation of the French, and that the necessary corollary of a dysfunctional government born in violence was that justice could not be readily obtained. The mechanisms to enforce it simply did not exist. His letters constantly urged the American government to show restraint in its dealings with France and to make no threats to break relations. Morris pointed out that those who chose to take advantage of the enormous potential benefits of trading with a country at war must also bear the equally increased risks. Thomas Paine would tell one group of angry American captains that Morris had told him that those who "had thrown themselves into the lion's mouth" had to "get out of it as best they could." The captains then denounced Morris. But he was quite right.

The two years that Morris remained in Paris after Louis's fall were a psychological ordeal of a type that few American diplomats—certainly not Jefferson—have had to endure. "People abroad can form no Idea of what passes here nor do I think any force of Description would convey it," Morris wrote to Thomas Pinckney during the Terror, which began in September 1793 with the ruthless Law of Suspects and continued until the fall of Robespierre at the end of July 1794. The Committee of Public Safety was now in command of the country and of the war, and brutal repression of dissent or suspected dissent became the order of the day in Paris and in the country's *départements*. Paris during this time little resembled the city that had beguiled Franklin, Jefferson, and William Short. On Christmas Eve 1792, Morris sent Robert Morris his good wishes for what "is with you a festive Season. I write from a Place deserted by its former Inhabitants where in almost every Countenance you can mark the Traces of present Woe and of dismal Forebodings."

Gouverneur Morris was repeatedly required to make difficult choices that he knew could leave people to the misery of the prisons and the possibility of the guillotine. With a hostile government now in power, failure to remain within the limits of international law in his official acts would have destroyed his ability to help those legally under his purview—that is, Americans. He could do little to help the French and British who came to him for help, though he did all he could. He himself was in danger; those who patrolled the streets and sent people to prison for merely appearing "suspect" were ignorant of the concept of diplomatic immunity. Morris was arrested more than once, and neighborhood "commissioners" tried to search his house, which he refused to permit.

Moreover, Morris did his duties with virtually no support from his own government, other than the help he received from the few American consuls in France. This was partly due to the disruption of mail service, but it is also a fact that Jefferson wrote him very rarely during that two-year-long period of desperation. For reasons that had to do entirely with American politics of the 1790s and nothing to do with the true situation in France, Jefferson was increasingly adamant in his support of the French Revolution—whatever that meant by this time, with the initial reformers and their proposals all violently destroyed and the subsequent governments bearing no resemblance to the dictates of the constitution of 1791. The real news from France was impossible to reconcile with the view Jefferson was determined to take, and so he clearly found it preferable to say nothing to Morris. As Morris wryly commented to Pinckney, "[o]ur Secretary of State seems much attached to Brevity, and reminds me of a Bromide of his Predecessor [Franklin], that least said is soonest mended."

On his side, Morris provided a steady output of dispatches to Jefferson and President Washington, including, as usual, many accurate predictions of subsequent events in France, both in the short and the long terms. But Morris's government did not grasp the difficulties he faced in dealing with the French government. The constant stream of complaints about him that reached America—and the rhapsodic letters from men such as Thomas Paine about the course of the Revolution—makes that lack of appreciation somewhat understandable. Morris realized this. "[I]f I get through this mission honorably, it will be a master-piece," he wrote to Robert Morris in June 1793; "and yet nine out of ten will say, that it was the easiest thing in nature."

The first issue that confronted Morris after King Louis was deposed was whether to recognize the new government. After Louis's fall, the Legislative Assembly declared the constitution suspended and named a Girondin "Provisory Executive Council" to run affairs and oversee election of delegates to a national convention that would implement the new Republic; the Republic was officially declared in the third week of September. "The present Executive is just born and may perhaps be stifled in the Cradle," Morris wrote to Jefferson on August 16. However, much as he detested the new regime, his advice to the American government was practical. He told Jefferson that he believed that prompt recognition was appropriate and indeed mandatory, and that he did not think he should leave France. Doing so

> would look like taking Part against the late Revolution and I am not only unauthoriz'd in this Respect but I am bound to suppose that if the great Majority of the Nation adhere to the new Form the United States will approve thereof because in the first Place we have no Right to prescribe to this Country the Government they shall adopt and next because the Basis of our own Constitution is the indefeasible Right of the People to establish it.

Jefferson would agree with this, as well as Morris's view that America should stand by its treaties with France. In fact, the U.S. government determined to declare its neutrality in the widening European war, something the French actually preferred over military support, since America could continue to ship goods to France under the protection of international neutrality laws.

Morris also directed William Short in the Hague to make a debt payment to the French that was agreed to just days before the king fell. Short resisted. He considered the new regime illegitimate and feared that he would be held accountable in America. Morris finally wrote impatiently to the recalcitrant Short: "Now I will not enter into any Question respecting the Competency of the present Government. The Corner Stone of our own Constitution is the Right of the People to establish such Government as they think proper. . . . I think it proper to adhere to the original Nature and Form of the present Payment."

When at last the payment was made, however, the Girondins—including his former business competitor, Clavière, now restored as finance minister—gave Morris no credit for making it but instead demanded more payments, ones not yet scheduled by the American government. When Morris pointed out that he did not have the authority to do what the Girondins desired, they sent the first of many requests for his recall to America. Morris suspected, probably correctly, that corruption was behind their demands for money. Nonetheless, he was concerned that the hostility of the new government would make him unable to perform his duties as minister, so he undertook a surprising countermeasure. He sent a man named Piquet, who had replaced Brémond as his principal source of intelligence, to visit the head of the attack on the Tuileries, General Westermann. Piquet apparently knew Westermann, and convinced him, undoubtedly by bribery, to write a letter on Morris's behalf to the Girondin foreign minister. The notion of Morris obtaining a reference letter from the man who led the massacre on August 10 is bizarre, but Westermann's letter is in the

French foreign ministry archives. How useful it was is debatable, but foreign minister LeBrun replied politely to Westermann that he would "profit" from the information.

The lack of input from his own government made Morris very uneasy. He wrote to George Washington at the end of October 1792 that he had repeatedly asked Jefferson for "positive instructions and orders for my government. I need not tell you, Sir, how agreeable this would be to me, and what a load it would take from my mind." At the same time, he told Washington, he was willing to be sacrificed if it suited America's foreign policy needs to disavow him.

Morris had no faith that those in power at the moment would remain in control; he described to Alexander Hamilton the dangerous tension between the Girondins and radical Montagnards of the Assembly:

> There are two Parties here. The one consists of about half a dozen and the other of fifteen or twenty who are at Dagger's Drawing. Each Claims the Merit of having begotten the young Republic upon the Body of the Jacobine Club and notwithstanding the Dispute is very loud and open the People is as fond of the Child as if it were its Own. But this has a Relation to antient Manners for there has been a Practice here from Time whereof there is no Memory of Man to the contrary viz that one Set of Men were employ'd in getting children for another Set. . . .

It is not worth while," he added, "to detail the Characters of those now on the Stage because they must soon give Place to others."

Yet, although Morris was utterly frank about his misgivings, the Girondins were mistaken in assuming that he would try to turn the American government against the new regime. He accepted the advent of the new Republic with his usual mixture of mildly hopeful idealism tempered with hardheaded skepticism. "[T]he great decided effective Majority is now for the Republic," he told Jefferson in late October 1792, but whether it would endure for even six months "must depend on the Form of Government which shall be presented by the Convention" and whether it could "strike out that happy Mean which secures all the Liberty which Circumstances will admit of combin'd with all the Energy which the same Circumstances require." In the meantime, he predicted, "we shall have, I think, some sharp struggles which will make many men repent of what they have done, when they find with Macbeth, that they have but taught bloody instructions, which return to plague the inventor."

Among the casualties of the king's downfall was Lafayette. In the face of his troops' defiance, he deserted the army on August 19 and fled towards Holland, only to be captured by the Austrians, who considered him a principal author of the Revolution and promptly sent him to the Prussian fortress of Wesel. He wrote to the three American ministers in Europe and, to their mortification, begged them to demand his release as an American citizen. There was not a legal leg to stand on with this claim, and they all knew it. Still, they did everything they could to help him—to little avail. He remained in prison for five years.

Many of Morris's friends escaped France, including Monciel, Malouet, and Moleville. Adèle obtained forged passports for herself, her son, Moleville, and her husband by bribing an official of the Paris commune, undoubtedly using money from Morris. She went to London. Her husband remained in France and would eventually be imprisoned and executed. Talleyrand, whose skills would always be for sale, traded a draft of a public statement justifying August 10 to the famous radical Danton in exchange for a passport. He, too, then left for England.

On September 2 Morris heard that "the Enemy are at the Gates of Paris, which cannot be true. . . . I observe that this Proclamation produces Terror and Despair among the People." The immediate result of the panic was the September Massacres, a "Week of uncheck'd Murders" in the city's prisons, where all "those who were confin'd, either on the accusation or Suspicion of Crimes"—many of them priests who had refused to renounce allegiance to the pope—were slaughtered. The British ambassador saw the scene and wrote to his superiors that the "kennel [the gutter of the prison] was swimming with blood, and a bloody track was traced from the prison to the Abbaye door, where they had dragged these unfortunate people." Morris told Jefferson: "Madame de Lamballe [one of Marie Antoinette's closest friends] was I believe the only Woman kill'd, and she was beheaded and emboweled, the Head and Entrails were paraded on Pikes thro the Street and the body dragged after them. . . . Monsieur de Montmorin was among those slain at the Abbey."

Jefferson, however, who now saw the struggle in France as critical to America's future as a republic, was determined to be sanguine. A few months later, having heard of the events of August 10 and the September massacres, he wrote a famous letter reproving William Short for criticizing the overthrow of the monarchy:

> In the struggle which was necessary, many guilty persons fell without the forms of trial, and with them some innocent. These I deplore as much as any body, and shall deplore some of them to the day of my death. But I deplore them as I should have done had they fallen in battle. . . . The liberty of the whole earth was depending on the issue of the contest, and was ever such a prize won with so little innocent blood?

Morris felt otherwise. "I will not pretend to describe what I wish to forget, and I fear also that a just Picture would be attributed rather to the Glow of Imagination than the lively coloring of Nature," he wrote Robert Morris. The strain was telling on Gouverneur, and he was ill for most of October. Paris was not safe, even for a diplomat, and he began to look for a safe haven outside the city. He found one in the small village of Seineport, about four hours' drive by carriage—twenty miles—from his official residence in the city, and took up residence there in April 1793. The house had gardens and orchards that needed to be tended and thus provided Morris with a welcome relief from his difficult duties. The previous summer he had hired a secretary, young Henry W. Livingston, who stayed behind at the legation. Jefferson approved the move.

During the fall of 1792, the tide turned for the French military in its fight against the invading Austrian and Prussian coalition. On September 22, the day after the National Convention declared France a Republic, Dumouriez triumphed over the Prussians at the Battle of Valmy in the northeast corner of France. In November, on his way to invade the Austrian Netherlands, Dumouriez beat the Austrians at the battle of Jemappes in Belgium.

Yet there was no parallel improvement in France's internal affairs. In early October, Brissot was expelled from the Jacobin Club. "You will see by the Gazettes," Morris commented to Jefferson, "that there is the same Enmity between the present Chiefs which prevailed heretofore against those whom they considered as their common Enemies, and if either of the present Parties should get the better, they would probably again divide; for Party like Matter is divisible ad infinitum." In early December 1792, in a letter to Thomas Pinckney, Morris penned his most eloquent appraisal of the tragic turn of the Revolution:

Success as you will see, continues to crown the French Arms, but it is not our Trade to judge from Success. . . . You will soon learn that the Patriots hitherto adored were but little worthy of the Incense they received. The Enemies of those who now reign treat them as they did their Predecessors and as their Successors will be treated. Since I have been in this Country, I have seen the Worship of many Idols and but little [illegible] of the true God. I have seen many of those Idols broken, and some of them beaten to Dust. I have seen the late Constitution in one short Year admired as a stupendous Monument of human Wisdom and ridiculed as an egregious Production of Folly and Vice. I wish much, very much, the Happiness of this inconstant People. I love them. I feel grateful for their Efforts in our Cause and I consider the Establishment of a good Constitution here as the principal Means, under divine Providence, of extending the blessings of Freedom to the many millions of my fellow Men who groan in Bondage on the Continent of Europe. But I do not greatly indulge the flattering Illusions of Hope, because I do not yet perceive that Reformation of Morals without which Liberty is but an empty Sound.

Meanwhile, the royal family remained imprisoned. In late October, Morris wrote to President Washington that he was sure their fate was sealed, for "History informs us that the Passage of dethroned Monarchs is short from the Prison to the Grave." In December, the convention voted to try Louis for treason, and on January 16, 1793, he was sentenced to death. "To a Person less intimately acquainted than you are with the History of human Affairs," Morris wrote to Jefferson, "it would seem strange that the mildest monarch who ever fill'd the French Throne, One who is precipitated from it precisely because he would not adopt the harsh measures of his Predecessors, a Man whom none can charge with a Criminal or Cruel Act, should be prosecuted as one of the most nefarious Tyrants that ever disgraced the Annals of human nature."

Morris hoped the execution would backfire, but there was no great outcry in France over Louis's death. The execution did, however, heighten the tension between England and France. On February 1, 1793, France declared war on England; a month later, it declared war on Spain. "The present prospects are dreadful," Morris wrote to Washington on the eve of late-February food riots in Paris.

> [T]he disorganized state of the government appears to be irremediable. . . . How all this will end, God only knows, but I fear it will end badly. I will not speak of my own situation; you will judge that it is far from pleasant. I could be popular, but that would be wrong. The different parties pass away like the shadows in a magic lantern, and to be well with any one of them, would in a short period become the cause of unquenchable hatred with the others.

In mid-March, Dumouriez was defeated by the Austrians at the Battle of Neerwinden, ending for the moment France's hopes of taking the Low Countries. Dumouriez had never been a genuine republican, just extremely ambitious. He had hoped to march back on Paris after a victory and seize control of the convention, now increasingly dominated by the radical Montagnards (extremist Jacobins from the Paris Jacobin Club). But after the defeat at Neerwinden, his troops would not follow him, and so he defected to the Austrians. The resurgent fear of invasion led the convention to order the establishment of municipal surveillance committees throughout France to keep an eye on foreigners and suspects. The

Revolutionary Tribunal had been established in March to examine crimes against the state, and in mid-April *assignats* were decreed to be the required currency. Parisians began to demand price controls, and seizing the political opportunity, the radical Montagnards in the Assembly obtained the first Law of the Maximum in early May, setting price limits on pain of death.

The provinces were also in turmoil. A civil war in the Vendée region erupted in March 1793. Morris reported that enforcement of the decree for conscripting a third of a million men had "met with serious opposition" in some places. The convention dispatched new and powerful Jacobin Montagnard representatives-on-mission throughout France to put the country, by any means possible, on a war footing.

In Paris, the Jacobin Montagnards and Girondins were now at each other's throats. The Girondins used the last of their strength in the convention to send up their archenemy, the famous Montagnard Marat, for trial, but in late April he was acquitted by the Revolutionary Tribunal. The Girondins then publicly denounced the conspiracies they knew were underway to topple them, but their threats had the same effect as the Brunswick Manifesto, backfiring badly. On June 2, after several false starts, about one hundred thousand people surrounded the convention while it considered a petition to decree the arrest of thirty principal Girondin deputies. Cowed by the crowds, the convention did so. The purge exacerbated the civil war. Marseilles and Bordeaux followed Lyons in rebellion against the Jacobins, and by mid-June over sixty of the *départements* had rebelled.

The victorious Jacobins worked quickly to produce a new constitution, but it was never implemented. The civil war and military reversals continued. The shortage of food did not improve. In early

July 1793, the Dantonists lost domination of the Committee of Public Safety to the group that was to remain in power until the end of the Terror. Robespierre, who had great influence with the Jacobins and the *sans-culottes,* was one of the new members. His election came the day after the surrender of Valenciennes to the Austrians and the passage of a draconian law against hoarding for which the only penalty was death. The *Levée en Masse,* calling the entire country into the war, was issued at the end of August, just a few days before the port of Toulon fell to the British.

"The present government is evidently a despotism both in principle and practice," Morris wrote to George Washington. "The Convention now consists of only a part of those who were chosen to frame a constitution. These, after putting under arrest their fellows, claim all power, and have delegated the greater part of it to a *Committee of Public Safety.*" It was now "an emphatical phrase in fashion among the patriots that *terror is the order of the day.*"

The fear—the Terror—had begun. Morris grasped its nature clearly, and with great accuracy he predicted its inevitable effects:

> [W]hatever may be the lot of France in remote futurity . . . it seems evident that she must soon be governed by a single despot. Whether she will pass to that point through the medium of a triumvirate, or other small body of men, seems as yet undetermined. I think it most probable that she will. A great and awful crisis seems to be near at hand. A blow is, I am told, meditated which will shroud in grief and horror a guilty land. Already the prisons are surcharged with persons, who consider themselves victims.

The "blow" Morris mentioned may have been the Committee's order, sent in mid-October 1793, to Lyons. Lyons had been subdued by the Jacobins, and the Committee's representative there was instructed to destroy the city for having dared to make "war on liberty," which was how the Jacobins described any opposition to the revolutionary government. By November, large-scale executions had begun. Morris might also have been referring to the *noyades* in Nantes, which also took place in October: these were mass drownings of perhaps two thousand men, women, and children, mostly Vendéans. October 1793 also saw the execution of Marie Antoinette. "Insulted during her trial, and reviled in her last moments, she behaved with dignity throughout," Morris wrote to Washington.

On October 31, 1793, twenty-one Girondins—including Morris's adversary and Paine's friend, Brissot de Warville, whom Jefferson had called "a true disciple of liberty"—went to the guillotine.

As the country churned in civil war, many suffered, including Americans and American ships and crews, and the dysfunctional government made Morris's efforts to help them often fruitless. The war had brought out French privateers who wasted little time on legal niceties in choosing their prey and who were often abetted by corrupt port officials. Although the American treaty with France called both sides to honor the international legal principle of "free ships make free goods"—that is, a neutral ship's cargo could not be seized unless it contained contraband—both the French and British were soon claiming the right to make such seizures on the basis of the other party's violation of the principle. A typical case was the *Laurence,* which had departed South Carolina with rice and indigo intended for delivery in Britain. It was seized and forced into port in France, where it remained trapped by the efforts of its captors to manipulate local officials and the National Convention into passing measures retroactively authorizing the seizure. Facilitated by rich bribes, these ploys were successful, and Morris's repeated protests to the French foreign minister were useless.

American crews also suffered. In one instance, *The Little Cherub,* an American ship that had departed Havre with a passport, was boarded by the crew of a French privateer. The captain declared to Morris that they had been "very ill treated, although they made no resistance; and that the French having entire possession of the American ship, one of them seized the second mate by the collar, and without the slightest provocation blew his brains out." In response to Morris's protests, the Committee of Public Safety ordered arrests and a trial, but "the Person who committed the Murder has however been acquitted on the Testimony of his Companions in direct Contradiction to that of the American Master and Crew," Morris wrote Jefferson in August.

Americans were also caught in the net when, in order to punish Bordeaux for its support of the Girondins, the National Convention declared an embargo on the port in the late summer of 1793. It remained in place through the following spring, and by late November the American consul reported to Morris that there were ninety-two American ships trapped there. "It has, at length, produced the greatest distress," Morris told Jefferson. "The crews have consumed their provisions. The merchants will be saddled with heavy loss and cost. I have made reiterated applications; but the situation of that city has prevented the *Comité de Salut Public* from a direct interference."

Although Morris's letters make it clear that he was unstinting in his protests about these violations of treaty and law, the government was consumed with the civil war, the war with Europe, and with the prodigious task of administering a fractured country. Morris described the government to Jefferson as "omnipotent in some cases [but] in others, not merely feeble, but enslaved." He did not threaten American retaliation, nor did he encourage his government to do so. Even "in the best Regulated Governments," he wrote to Jefferson, "it is difficult to prevent the Violation of the Rights of neutral Powers." These moderate comments influenced Jefferson and Washington to tone down their public statements protesting French violations of American merchant shipping neutrality.

Morris said the same things to the Americans in France. He told Swan that "the Sufferings of my unfortunate countrymen who are brought into the [F]rench ports give me very great pain. I have explained so fully to the Ministers of the Republic all the mischievous Consequences of that injurious Treatment that my Powers of Reason and Language can go no farther." This was cold comfort to the distressed Americans. Many of them refused to believe that their minister could not demand immediate redress from a country that was an ally. A deputation of captains from the ships trapped at Bordeaux came to Paris and, ignoring Morris's advice, went directly to the National Convention, where they obtained a decree that seemed to promise relief; but as he had predicted, it was almost immediately reversed. They foolishly repeated his comments about the dysfunctional state of the government to French officials, with the inevitable effect of injuring his effectiveness with no benefit to their own situation. And they sent complaints about Morris back to the United States. It is difficult to imagine what the captains thought Morris could have done to break the Bordeaux embargo. His papers establish that he was as diligent as he was accused of being negligent.

Americans who were arrested also sent to him for help. The arrests were generally arbitrary—it was enough to be a foreigner to be suspect—but difficult to undo. "Persons in prison are so numerous that none can get out because in the multitude of applications there is no time to examine any particular complaint," he wrote. Morris's continued protests on their behalf usually had an effect, but, naturally, for those in prison any wait at all was dreadful. A typical example is that of young William Hoskins, who had been arrested in Calais after disembarking from an American ship. He wrote Morris on January 1, 1794, from the Luxembourg prison in Paris:

> Penetrated to the heart with the thought of an arrestation and the fatigue already experienced from my journey from Calais, I scarcely know what to write. . . . I hope you will have the kindness to attend to my subject without delay, this I flatter myself of; yes, Sir, when you imagine to yourself my present situation, lodged in a chamber with two persons who are extremely sick of a fever & nothing to sleep on the last evening, without a farthing to purchase the necessaries of life, when this fact is told you I am persuaded the sympathy for a fellow countryman will excite your exertions as well as your pity. . . . [D]o not delay for I am already sick—

Morris wrote and visited the foreign minister repeatedly on Hoskins's behalf and kept Hoskins apprised of these efforts. After about a month, Hoskins was finally freed.

Others asked Morris to violate international law. "I have had Applications to grant Privileges of the American Flag to vessels owned by [F]renchmen and others," he wrote to Robert Morris. "Some of the Applicants were offended at my Refusal *of that trifling favor.*" He was repeatedly forced to refuse passports, explaining that he could not issue them unless certain that the recipient was properly eligible; "the Government in that Jealousy which is inspired by so many open and secret Enemies would cease to protect the American Citizens possess'd of Certificates from me if I ceased my Vigilance in granting them," he told one petitioner.

Yet Morris gave what help and comfort he could. Many people, not just American citizens, and many of them strangers, turned to him. For non-Americans, he did not make use of his official capacity but worked privately, sending news to relatives and getting money to those who needed it. And though the record is fragmented, it is evident that when Morris left France there were many who felt nothing but profound gratitude toward him. One woman whose husband was taken to prison after August 10 while she remained under house arrest was allowed to speak to the foreign diplomats to ask their help. "The person who received her with the most kindness was the American minister, Mr. Morris," a friend later recorded. Another woman wrote Morris that she thought of his legation on the Rue de la Planche as the *planche* (board) that was saving her from drowning after a shipwreck.

Morris was even solicitous towards the ungrateful William Short regarding the imprisonment of his lover Rosalie de la Rochefoucauld. He wrote him regularly with what little he could learn, and he did his best to get letters in and out of the prison. He arranged for Robert Morris to temporarily manage the Rochefoucaulds' estate in Haiti. "Were it in my power to be of any use to them believe me I would have flown to their relief," he told the agonized Short, "but there is nothing to be done and patience alone can assuage the misery of many thousands."

He also helped Madame de Lafayette. He worked with her on petitions for her husband's release to the king of Prussia, and he sent ten thousand florins of his own money to Lafayette in his prison camp, for which he was later reimbursed by the American government. She asked Morris to help cover her husband's "debts of honor" and Morris did so with one hundred thousand livres of his own money—twice his annual salary—the "utmost which my fortune will permit, and I am indeed incommoded in getting the money to fulfill my Engagements," he told Pinckney, asking him not to tell anyone else. He did not ask reimbursement for this from his government. It would be many years before he was repaid by the Lafayettes, and then it was only in part—and grudgingly given.

Morris's compassion toward Madame de Lafayette was unfazed by her hostility. In one letter to Pinckney he asked the minister to forward one of Lafayette's letters to him from prison so that Morris could give it to his wife, "for it will be a great Consolation to her to see his writing. Poor Lady she is in great affliction." She was encouraged by others whom Morris disapproved of to take more desperate steps, including providing money to help Lafayette try to escape. Morris believed this step too dangerous, and she reproached him bitterly. "I will not injure a man for the Sake of appearing to be his Friend," he responded.

In the spring of 1794, there was a new spate of arrests and executions in Paris, known as the Great Terror. Louis's elderly counselor, Malesherbes, whom Morris had liked from his first days in Paris, was guillotined on April 22 after watching his daughter, son-in-law, and granddaughter precede him up the bloody stairs of the scaffold. On June 10 Morris received word that Madame de Lafayette had been arrested and was being brought to Paris. He drafted a carefully propitiating petition on her behalf, emphasizing her importance to Americans. She was not released until January 1795, after Morris had been replaced by James Monroe, but her sisters and Madame de Staël gave Morris full credit for having saved her from execution.

In March 1794, Morris wrote sadly to Robert Morris:

> I believe that my residence here has been of little use, but that is not my fault. If the present Secretary of State should take the trouble of reading over my letters from the beginning, he will find that I have given regularly, for months beforehand, an account of what would happen. If credit was not given to my predictions, it is not my fault. As to my conduct here, I will neither praise it nor excuse it, but confine myself to the sincere wish that my successor, whoever he may be, may act with more wisdom in a situation less critical; and for the rest, I leave it to fortune, which is but another name for providence knowing that the world judges only from events, and, of course, that the General or Statesman, who gains one brilliant affair, is more applauded than he who resists with small force or assistance, and in a dangerous situation, through the course of a long campaign.
>
> I am ashamed of having said so much of myself even to you. . . .

This letter is one of Morris's few acknowledgements of the strain he had been under. Much as he wanted to be free of the terrible onus of responsibility, he never requested to be relieved of his position. He strongly believed that the American government should not even discuss French requests for his recall, because doing so undermined his effectiveness in performing his duties. He knew that such requests had been made, though he apparently did not know the details—nor did he know that Washington had intended to consent and was only forestalled by the constant changes in the French regime and the lack of an acceptable replacement.

Although his government would never even partially appreciate what he had endured, it is clear that Morris rendered it extraordinary service. Theodore Roosevelt wrote that Morris's time as minister "stands by itself in diplomatic history." The evidence supports that claim and refutes those who persist in representing Morris as a reactionary who damaged American relations with France.

Yet he was, finally, recalled. The justification given to Morris was that the French had requested it as a quid pro quo for the recall of the French minister to America, the provocative and imprudent Edmund Genet. This explanation has been accepted by some historians at face value. But in fact it had little to do with it: the real reasons were myriad. Perhaps foremost was the accumulation of complaints about him from Americans in France, beginning with William Short's unceasing efforts to influence Jefferson against Morris's appointment.

Thomas Paine also had written Jefferson to denounce the selection of Morris. They had never been friends, though Paine never hesitated to ask Morris for money, which Morris gave him, knowing he would never be repaid. Morris had always admired Paine's talent as a writer, but he found him irritating, noting that although Paine "has an excellent Pen to write he has but an indifferent Head to think." Paine had worn out his welcome in Britain by writing a scathing rebuttal to Edmund Burke's *Reflections on the Revolution in France.* He left Britain as a pariah in 1792 and arrived in France a hero, accepting French citizenship and election to the national convention as a deputy.

Paine had been a close friend of the Girondin leaders, and their fall from power and execution in October 1793 meant that his own days were numbered. He was arrested in December and taken to the Luxembourg Prison. When the petitions of his French and

American friends had no effect, he reluctantly turned to Morris, insisting that Morris demand his release on the basis that as an American the French had no right to arrest him. His outrage that he had been arrested, given the fate of the Girondins and of thousands of other French citizens far more innocent, is remarkable; and when Morris's letter to the head of foreign affairs was rejected, Paine was vitriolic, blaming Morris and threatening him with retaliation. He utterly rejected the French position that by accepting a place in the convention as a French citizen he had put himself under the laws of the French Republic, a point Morris could not dispute. Morris told Paine's friends that Paine would be better advised to lie low: "[W]hether he be considered as a Frenchman, or as an American, he must be amenable to the tribunals of France for his conduct while he was a Frenchman, and he may see in the fate of the Brissotins that to which he is exposed." Paine was not released until after the fall of Robespierre and the end of the Terror. He went to stay with James Monroe in Paris, where he spent much of his time drinking and writing a bitter denunciation of Washington and Morris.

Another concerted effort to have Morris recalled was made by a motley group of profiteers that included William Stephens Smith—John Adams's son-in-law and disappointed contender for the position of minister to London—and the scoundrel Stephen Sayre. Sayre had had an odd career that included a 1775 arrest on suspicion of plotting to kidnap George III, a brawl with John Paul Jones after he had insulted Jones in a pub, and various stints in debtor's prison in London. He and Smith were the unlikely friends of the dashing Venezuelan Francisco de Miranda (1756–1816), who sought their support for his plan to oust the Spanish from his country. Miranda also worked to interest the British government in this project, and Smith and Sayre hoped to profit from associated war contracts. The British were interested, but when nothing significant materialized, Miranda joined the French military, hoping the French would be interested in spreading their revolution to Spain's colonies.

Sayre presented this scheme to the receptive Girondin ministry, suggesting that they could use the balance of the American debt to France and promising rake-offs for supply contracts. Morris was considered an obstacle to this plan, and Sayre and Smith did their best to have him removed. Sayre circulated pamphlets in France and America denouncing Morris, and Smith—who knew Morris and dined at his house while in Paris—met with Jefferson and Washington in early 1793 to tell them that the French ministry distrusted Morris and wanted him recalled. Washington was convinced that Morris should go, and it was only the uncertainty about who would replace him that kept Morris in place. Jefferson refused to serve as his replacement; nor did he take the opportunity to ask for his recall.

What was probably the decisive incident leading to Morris's recall took place in November 1793 at his residence at Seineport. Local officials with a warrant entered the house over Morris's protests and arrested Madame de Damas, the wife of a former officer in the American Revolution who had been a friend of Washington. Her husband had emigrated to Italy but she had remained in France, hoping to protect her property. She had taken refuge with Morris some time the previous spring. In the fall, at the beginning of the Terror, the National Convention had passed a Law of Suspects that authorized arrests on the very broad grounds of being an "enemy of liberty." Madame de Damas's sister and brother-in-law had already been arrested, and her brother-in-law had been guillotined.

Her arrest presented Morris with a difficult problem. He knew that there was no basis on which to dispute her arrest, for she was a French citizen. What he could argue, however, was that the forcible entry of his house to seize her was a violation of *his* rights under international law, and he made this point repeatedly to the French foreign minister, suggesting that the proper remedy would be to let her return to his house and stay under his recognizance. Well aware that he was on delicate ground, he asked the Committee of General Surety to "recall the principle which I believe is of importance to all nations, that the house of an ambassador or other minister is inviolable as the territory of his country." His measured words disguised deep outrage over this violation of America's extraterritorial rights, which he believed justified a diplomatic breach between France and America. He seriously considered leaving France, but as he later told Washington, he decided that he must stay in order to continue helping Americans who were in trouble there.

The Committee would not let Madame de Damas go. Nonetheless, they were concerned that Morris would use the incident as a reason to sever diplomatic relations, and they moved to request his recall in January 1794. The new French representative in America, Joseph Fauchet, was so instructed, but though the letter described Morris as "corrupt" and "perfidious" it did not instruct Fauchet to mention the de Damas affair, undoubtedly because the French government knew that Morris was in the right.

Morris had no reservations about what he had done and described his actions fully to Washington and Jefferson. As the wife of a former Revolutionary officer, just like Madame de Lafayette, Madame de Damas was entitled to all the efforts he could make within the limits of his authority. It seems very likely that his protests saved her from the guillotine. For her part, Madame de

Damas's opinion of Morris was obvious: immediately upon her release she returned to Seineport.

Fauchet presented a request for Morris's recall to the new secretary of state, Edmund Randolph, in early April 1794; he found the American government quite willing to comply. Randolph was propitiating, telling Fauchet that America "wanted to have only ministers the French approved of"; but Randolph's letter to Morris put the matter entirely on the basis of reciprocity for the American request to recall Fauchet's predecessor, Edmund Genet. It was not, he said to Morris, "from a dissatisfaction which the President has conceived at your conduct." On June 9, Fauchet wrote to the French government that James Monroe, "known as an honest man who desires the good of our country," would soon replace Morris.

The spring and summer of 1794 had been among the deadliest periods of the Revolution, with the Great Terror accelerating throughout the late spring. Morris reported to Randolph in the third week of July about tensions within and between the National Convention's governing Committee of Public Safety and the Committee of General Surety, as well as within the Paris Commune, the Paris governmental body that had often refused to obey the convention and had intimidated it by staging huge protests of angry mobs. The ferment, said Morris, "must lead to an explosion." Less than a week later, the expected explosion took place. On July 27, members of the Committee of Public Safety, including some with the most blood on their hands, turned on Robespierre and his followers in a session of the National Convention and procured a decree of arrest. The result was inevitable: within a day, Robespierre and his followers were dead. The Terror was over, and the Reaction had begun.

On July 29, Henry Livingston, who had received a New York paper with the news of Morris's recall and Monroe's appointment, notified Morris of the decision at Seineport. Monroe's timing would prove remarkable: he arrived in Paris on August 2, 1794, four days after Robespierre's death on the guillotine.

Morris was gracious to the new minister, though he must have been aware of the many attacks, public and private, that Monroe had made on him in America. He arranged for the Monroes to take over the lease of the legation, and he presented Monroe to the commissioners of foreign relations a week after his arrival. At Morris's suggestion, Monroe presented his credentials to the National Convention, where he was greeted with great acclaim. Yet Monroe would soon discover that "fine words are of little value," as Morris wrote to Washington, and that "something more is expected (and justly expected)" in America "for the many violences committed against our merchants." Morris would hear later that "Mr. Monroe found it difficult to change principles fast enough to keep pace with the changes in the French Government." Two years and four months after his triumphant reception, an angry and bitter Monroe would be recalled from France.

Morris's feelings on being relieved of his position were mixed; although he wrote to Short that he was thankful to be recalled, the circumstances troubled him. He wrote in his diary, "[S]o far as I am personally concerned at least I have the Consolation to have made no Sacrifice either of personal or national Dignity and I believe I should have obtain'd every Thing if the American Government had refused to recall me. I rejoice that I am no longer in the pitiful situation which I have so long endured. For the rest Experience must decide and I hope that events will be favorable to America." His preparations to leave took time, for he had acquired a considerable collection of fine objects while in Paris. (It included furniture—one of the chairs he bought, which Louis XVI used when he visited Marie Antoinette in her apartments, is on display at the New York Historical Society—silver, paintings, books, and more.) He was also delayed by the need for a passport. The government of the Thermidorean Reaction was as hostile to Morris as its predecessors, and they were unwilling to permit him to leave for Switzerland and then reenter to depart from Havre for America, as he had hoped to do. When he agreed to not reenter France, his passport was granted with insulting rapidity. On October 12 he left Paris for Seineport. Two days later he left Seineport for Switzerland.

Unfortunately for us, Morris's diary would never again include the rich detail of his years in Paris. This undoubtedly is a reflection of the toll that the ordeal took on him and possibly also the effect of the recall, which, though a huge relief, was also a great humiliation. As he drove in his carriage through the Alps, he seems to have been in something of a state of numbness. Aside from an occasional remark on the evidently bad effects of the Revolution and the war throughout France, he did not use the diary to ruminate on his experience but instead described, with an agriculturalist's eye, the landscape through which he was traveling. He was now subject to repeated attacks of gout, was often sick, and, during that first winter, clearly depressed. "Another Year is added to the many which have been lost in the abyss of eternal Duration . . ." he wrote on December 31, 1794, in Hamburg.

For several reasons, Morris decided to remain in Europe. He was determined to continue his efforts to free Lafayette, and he may also have been involved in British-sponsored efforts to restore a constitutional monarchy in France, though much research remains to be done in this area. He also hoped to complete a few major business deals (he would return to America in excellent financial shape). And, probably most important of all, there was Adèle.

They saw each other again in Germany in March 1795, after a gap of nearly two and a half years. While exiled in London, she had used her talent for writing to help support herself and her son, turning out a number of successful romantic novels. Talleyrand had also gone to London, but in 1794 the British government, suspicious that he was involved in a plan to promote an Irish rebellion, directed him to leave; regardless, he had probably done little to help Adèle. Morris undoubtedly gave her money, as did her other lover, young Lord Wycombe, but she wanted to return to the Continent and for a while agreed to chaperone the Duc d'Orléans, son of Morris's friend the *duchesse* and possible heir to the throne if a monarchy were restored in France. At her request, Morris acted as a surety for money to support him and leased a house for her in Altona, near Hamburg.

It is likely that Adèle reconsidered the relationship when Morris was recalled and effectively banished from returning to Paris, where she most wanted to be. Moreover, the circumstances of her husband's death—the gallant but unlucky Comte de Flahaut was executed after being accused of passing on counterfeit *assignats*—may well have poisoned their relationship. Their reunion in Hamburg was apparently not happy. Eventually, Morris left for London, but when he heard a year later that she had become engaged to the Portuguese ambassador to Denmark, he immediately left for Hamburg. Whether he proposed marriage or not (which seems unlikely), she did not marry DeSouza at that time. But she and Morris did not resume their relationship. In the fall of 1797, she said goodbye to him for the last time and left for France. He would remain a bachelor for the next ten years.

Two weeks after Adèle left, Lafayette was released. He would assert that the Austrians had honored the request of Napoleon, made during peace negotiations between the French and Austrians, to let him go. But Morris, who had for several years insistently lobbied the English and many others for Lafayette's release, attributed the release to his own efforts, though he said so only privately. Morris was present when Lafayette was freed. He advised him to avoid France and to consider emigrating to America where, he was sure, the American government would give him a pension; true to form, Lafayette ignored his advice.

Morris stayed in Europe for another year, traveling about Europe and writing commentaries on the Continental situation to Lord Grenville. Finally, in the fall of 1798, Morris left for America. He would never return to Europe.

CHAPTER THIRTEEN

RETURN TO AMERICA

GOUVERNEUR MORRIS ARRIVED IN NEW YORK IN LATE DECEMber and promptly threw himself—and a large amount of money—into rebuilding the neglected manor house at Morrisania and turning the farm into a productive enterprise. He also visited his old friends in the city and was brought up to date on the political thicket that enmeshed President John Adams.

From the beginning of the wars of the French Revolution, the United States had caromed between outrage at Britain and France. Both countries had used the expedience of war to attack American shipping, and the indifference of the British to Morris's mission to London meant that no progress had been made on completion of the peace treaty terms. With serious Indian problems on the frontiers, which Congress blamed on hostile British activities, and increasingly frequent British violations of the neutrality rights of American ships and British impressment of American sailors, the country was in an ugly mood.

In 1794, Washington had sent John Jay to talk to Lord William Grenville. He returned with a treaty that contained probably the best the United States could hope for at the time but which outraged the Republicans, including Jefferson and others, who viewed it as disgracefully submissive and, worse, as amounting effectively to choosing the British side over the French. Morris noted accurately that the treaty would prove a "Mill Stone" about Jay's neck; he thought it badly flawed but believed that it should still be approved by the Senate as a great deal better than nothing.

The treaty provided for the Northwest posts to be returned to American control by mid-1796; it opened trade in India to American ships, which would later prove quite profitable; and it granted indemnification for ships seized by the British navy. At the same time, the Americans agreed that the rule of "free ships, free goods," which protected their neutral shipping, would not apply to shipments to France. This was a high price to pay, and it infuriated the French, who were counting on American provisions for their war effort. James Monroe was a target of their outrage, though he was also incensed by the agreement and said so, leading to his recall.

The French used the Jay Treaty as an excuse to abandon restraint in capturing American ships on the high seas. In 1797, they issued a decree declaring American seamen on British ships to be "pirates" and subject to hanging. That year, a beleaguered John Adams sent commissioners to France to try and improve relations. They were met with an insulting demand for an enormous bribe—instigated by none other than the eternally avaricious Talleyrand, now minister of foreign affairs. The Americans refused to pay, and the commissioners returned home to report on what would be called the "XYZ" affair. The story sparked a wave of anti-French sentiment in America, which was fanned by the Federalists and led by Hamilton. By the spring of 1798 the United States was engaged in what would be called the "Quasi-War" with its former ally, to the mortification of the Republicans. The navy was authorized to seize French military vessels off the American coast, trade with France was suspended, and a provisional army was planned.

The army was a major political problem for a country that had revolted against Britain in part because of opposition to "standing armies." And the taxes imposed to support it were unpopular—in Morris's view, deservedly so. An aging Washington agreed to lead the army, but only if Hamilton was appointed his second in command. Adams resisted this, for he had had nothing but trouble with Hamilton and Hamilton's cronies in the cabinet since taking office. But eventually he was forced to yield, and Hamilton was made a general.

Morris had seen enough of war to believe that, in this case at least, it should be avoided at all costs. In the new, bitterly partisan climate of American politics, he was naturally a Federalist, though his positions were based on his analysis of individual issues rather than on his alignment with a particular clique. He did not always concur with Federalist views, and he remained good friends with many Republicans, including Robert R. Livingston, who had decamped from the Federalists when slighted by Hamilton.

Morris was enough troubled by the partisan tone of American politics to beg Washington in late 1799 to run for president in the next election. This plea has been characterized as an indication of how far Morris had become out of touch with the new republic, for Washington himself had been vilified without restraint by Republican newspapers and was now seen as a Federalist, despite his long effort to discourage the rise of parties and factionalism. Yet Morris knew all that; his letter to Washington expressed his hope that another Washington term would civilize debate and heal divisions.

But Washington could not come to the rescue. He was already in the grip of a fatal illness when Morris wrote, and he died at Mount Vernon on December 14, 1799. A few weeks later, at the request of the city of New York, Morris gave the eulogy for Washington, "the greatest and best of men"—and for an era that would never return.

In the meantime, war fever had ebbed. In response to American anger over the XYZ affair, the French had made peace overtures. Their push to end hostilities continued after Napoleon took complete power. To the outrage of the more zealous Federalists, Adams was receptive to their approaches, and the groundwork was laid for the 1800 Treaty of Mortefontaine and the end of the Quasi-War.

A few months after Washington's death, Morris agreed to fill the seat of a resigning New York senator. He had only been back in the United States for a year, so his decision to accept the position is an interesting one. Perhaps he wished to see how the system he had helped design was actually functioning, or to see the birth of the new seat of government in Washington, D.C., where Congress had moved at the end of 1799. Perhaps he had some political ambition left. In any event, the timing of his appointment allowed him to observe one of the first crises of the new Constitution: the election of 1800, in which John Adams went down to defeat and the nation teetered between Aaron Burr and Thomas Jefferson. It was a choice the Federalists had hoped never to have to make and a bitter irony for Hamilton, who found himself having to support his rival Jefferson in order to avoid the greater evil of Burr.

Morris's letters to his friends concerning Jefferson's victory reflected his resignation about the Federalists' loss of power, but he was far from indifferent when the new Congress, backed by Jefferson, moved to vacate the Judiciary Act of 1801. That act put the federal system in much easier reach for Americans by creating new district courts and, what is more important, creating circuit courts with permanent judges. No longer would Supreme Court justices "ride" the circuits. Morris had much more faith in federal courts than in state courts and strongly supported the act. The Republicans, however, were concerned with preventing the preservation of Federalist power through Federalist appointments to those judgeships, and they promptly sent up a nullifying bill. Morris spoke against it, giving what was described in a Washington newspaper as "the greatest display of eloquence ever exhibited in a deliberative body," but to no avail, and the bill was passed in March 1802.

Morris's public life came to an end at the beginning of March 1803, when the New York legislature elected DeWitt Clinton for the Senate. That summer—when it was too late for Morris to cast a vote—news came of the Louisiana Purchase, and Morris, who had long ago expressed a vision of an America that stretched from one sea to the other, was all in favor. He had greeted the earlier news that Spain had given Louisiana back to the French with great concern and had even encouraged the U.S. to seize Louisiana by military means. Buying it was far preferable, but his position put him at odds with the Federalists in Congress, who voted against the treaty on party lines.

With the country in the hands of the Republicans, whose national policies Morris largely despised, he was for the next decade glad to turn away from politics and to devote himself to life in New York. He made many trips to visit his large landholdings in the state, and the rugged conditions seem to have suited him well. The potential to shape the region's future growth in a way that contrasted with the unproductive husbandry and poverty that he had often observed in Europe gave him great pleasure, as did the sheer beauty of the landscape.

Two accomplishments stand out from this period: Morris's work in designing the layout of Manhattan, and the laying of groundwork for the Erie Canal. In 1807, Morris accepted an appointment by the state to a planning committee charged with creating a street plan that would control New York City's future growth. It took four years to complete the assignment, and the result was the logical and eminently practical north-south east-west lattice we know today, extending from what was designated 155th Street in Harlem to the base of Manhattan at Houston Street. Morris thereby demonstrated his disdain for the lovely sweeps and facets of Pierre L'Enfant's design for Washington, D.C., pursuing an esthetic of efficiency instead. Yet the purpose of the two designs was also different: Washington, in Jefferson's view, was to be a statement on the nature of the nation's government. New York had no such elevated destiny but was instead well on the way to being the nation's commercial center, and Morris as much as anyone did not underestimate its likely scope. His travels through Europe had revealed to him the inefficiencies caused by unstructured urban growth.

Morris's other great mission was the promotion of the Erie Canal. The canal was not a new idea. Canals had undoubtedly been discussed at the Morrisania dinner table in his childhood, and a friend of his grandfather had proposed a canal from Erie to the Hudson in 1729. Since his youth Morris had believed that canals would be a principal means by which America would become unified, and he recognized the tremendous commercial benefits the proposed Erie Canal would bring to New York City. Many years after the fact, General Morgan Lewis recalled evenings at General Philip Schuyler's headquarters in the winter of 1777, when they all listened to a youthful Morris "descanting with great energy on what he termed 'the rising glories' of America and how commerce and agriculture, facilitated by great watercourses," would promote these glories. He "announced in language highly poetic, and to which I cannot do justice, that at no very distant day, the waters of the great western inland seas would, by the aid of man, break through their barriers and mingle with those of the Hudson." Morris's study of the great canals of Europe, followed by his trips around upstate New York, intensified that conviction. In 1810 he accepted the chairmanship of the New York Board of Canal Commissioners.

DeWitt Clinton, who has generally been awarded the title of the father of the Erie Canal, clearly felt some uneasiness about Morris's role. His memoirs include letters from people involved in the early days of the canal that purport to show that Morris's conception of the canal—both in terms of its route and its engineering concept—was deeply flawed and impractical, and that his stubbornness actually delayed the entire project. After Clinton's memoir was published, however, Jared Sparks, Morris's first biographer, took issue with the letters and Clinton's conclusions. Sparks established that Morris had abandoned his original engineering concept when he became convinced that it was impractical, and he quoted a letter written by Stephen Van Rensselaer, a fellow canal commissioner, that called Morris the "father" of the canal.

Morris was certainly a principal force behind the project for many years. In 1811, he went with Clinton to Washington, D.C., in a vain attempt to obtain federal funding; when they failed, he told the New York government that the state should go it alone, as it eventually did. He remained heavily involved in the project until shortly before his death, reading engineering reports and writing budget estimates. He would not live to see it built—construction began in 1817 and was completed in 1825—but it would prove a marvel of engineering, 363 miles long, far longer than any canal in Europe. It was four feet deep and forty feet wide and dealt with a rise of nearly six hundred feet from the Hudson to Lake Erie through a series of eighty-three locks. It proved, as Morris had anticipated, a tremendous boost to prosperity for the United States and to westward development.

Morris's later years also included, at long last, marriage. It is not clear from his papers how many single women might have been interested in marrying the one-legged squire of Morrisania, but he either felt no reciprocal interest in them or, more likely, simply adhered to his long-expressed disinclination to marriage. This might seem surprising in a man who had consistently demonstrated respect and admiration for women, as well as the capacity to love, but in examining this aspect of Morris no letters or diary entries exist that permit us to do more than speculate. Morris's sense of his own worth as a husband, especially once he reached his fifties, an age considered elderly in those days, may have been minimal. But he could help Anne Randolph by marrying her, and he knew it.

The fascinating story of Anne Randolph has been discussed in several recent books. When Anne was only seventeen she went to live with her sister Judith and Judith's husband Richard Randolph at a Virginia plantation called Bizarre. She apparently became engaged there to Richard's brother Theodorick, and by her own account, she became physically involved with him a short while before his untimely death on February 14, 1792. Six months later, she apparently showed signs of being pregnant, and on the night of October 1, 1792, while she was visiting friends, witnesses later reported that they had heard screams. The remains of an infant were allegedly found a few days later on the grounds of the plantation, although this was not confirmed.

Theodorick's ill health contributed to the widespread rumor that Anne had borne a baby that was actually Richard's, and that it had been killed. Though he was not charged, Richard attempted to clear his name by demanding a trial; his defense attorney was the future chief justice John Marshall. The court concluded that the case had not been proved against Richard. Anne then returned to Bizarre to live with her sister and brother-in-law. The acquittal did nothing to dispel the cloud over her or to stop the gossip—Patsy Randolph, Jefferson's daughter, wrote to her father a rather ugly note that only "inconsiderable people" had believed the verdict of the court.

Anne's sister later turned against her; she was no longer welcome in the Randolph clan, though she stayed until around 1805 when the unceasing persecution by many, including her cousin, the brilliant but tormented John Randolph, became too much. Reared a Virginia gentlewoman, Anne was now forced to rely on her own resources. She apparently wandered from one position to another before arriving in New York in 1808, where Morris learned of her residence at a boarding house. He had actually met her when she was a young girl during his trip through Virginia after the Constitutional Convention. He had clearly heard something of the story about her, but his only concern in drawing close to her appears to have been the potential for scandal-mongering by the Republican party. In March 1809, he invited her to become his housekeeper—telling her that though he would pay her their relationship would be one of "friends," not employer and employee—and she accepted. One historian notes that this was quite practical of Morris, for he needed a reliable domestic hand to ease the burden of managing his large and bustling house, and Anne Randolph had been born and bred to just this sort of work.

Only eight months after she came to Morrisania, Morris married Anne—to the outrage of his many relatives who were counting on sharing in their aging relative's estate. This blow was compounded when she gave birth to a son, Gouverneur Morris, in February 1813. Morris was well aware of the distress his decision gave his nephews and others. He found it humorous, though he would have been angered by their efforts after his death to malign Anne and challenge the distribution of his estate. It was typical of Morris, but at the same time extraordinary, that he gave her a prenuptial agreement that guaranteed her a monthly income on his death and provided that the income should be increased by over a quarter if she remarried, "to defray the increased expenditure which might attend that connexion." It would have grieved Morris to know that instead of the comfortable security he had intended for her, Anne would spend the decades after his death struggling to free the estate from liens caused by Morris's nephew David Ogden, who had fraudulently cosigned Morris's name to several enormous loans and then defaulted.

While Morris's taciturnity late in life makes it difficult to know the details of his emotional attachment to Anne Randolph, there are hints of his feelings, including one tender letter he wrote to her in verse that began by directing her to "Kiss for me, my love, our charming boy." Anne accompanied him on his trips to visit his lands in upstate New York, even though the traveling was arduous, and he must have appreciated the company. They read books together. And to have a wife tending him rather than servants in his last months of illness must have been a solace. On her side, Anne Randolph Morris's appreciation of and love for her remarkable husband is clear. On the last page of Morris's diary, written in October 1816, shortly before he died, Anne later scrawled a raw, grief-stricken paragraph—"Oh my adored, my best of Husbands," she wrote, "Had I been told this was to be the last morning we should leave our chamber together—that [this was to be] the last night we should reenter it together—I should have thought my Heart would Burst."

Morris's work on the canal and his domestic happiness during the last years of his life did not entirely distract him from politics and the approach of war with Britain—the War of 1812. He had, despite his approval of the Louisiana Purchase, little brief for Jefferson as president, or for his successor Madison. In 1805, he wrote to a correspondent:

> That our administration is too feeble is I believe too true. What you say of their Chief [Jefferson] is curious. When he told you we have the choice of enemies [France or England], he stated a fact applicable at all times to all countries, since any blundering blockhead may make a war; but when he acknowledged that we have not a choice of friends he pronounced the surest satire on himself, since this misfortune can be attributed only to a series of false and foolish measures.
>
> The position of our country enables her in general to take the part which may best suit her interest. . . . [T]he exercise of a little common sense would not only have preserved us from our present ridiculous condition but placed us perfectly at ease both at home and abroad.

Morris was referring to both Jefferson's and Madison's ineffective efforts to protect the United States from the fallout of the European war. There had been a series of French and British efforts to blockade each other from receiving American ships, as well as British court rulings that effectively ended the American carrying trade out of the British West Indies. In 1807, Jefferson convinced Congress to pass an embargo in retaliation against both nations, locking American ships into U.S. ports. The embargo lasted fifteen months, through the end of Jefferson's time in office, and its effects were dramatic: the federal revenue was cut to ribbons, and with the end of trade into the port cities, the American economy was hit hard. Morris was disgusted, describing the embargo as an act so "hostile to freedom" that even a monarchy like the British government would never have proposed imposing it on its people.

To Morris, the embargo and its successors, by which Jefferson and Madison tried to use rewards and punishments to control the European powers, were pathetic. These measures demonstrated American weakness, particularly military weakness after a decade of Republican cost-cutting, and an inexcusable lack of understanding of the European situation. England was engaged in a battle for its survival: Napoleon was steadily taking the Continent and made no secret of his intention to add the British to those under his dominion. France naturally had every reason to interrupt Britain's access to the rich storehouse on the other side of the Atlantic, and to take those goods for their own war effort. Britain had reason to use every strategy available to stop them.

The issue of impressment of American sailors was espoused as a matter of national honor, but here again Morris's views were pragmatic. British sailors were deserting in British ports in significant numbers and signing on to American merchant ships, a blow to the British navy's morale and one which American courts did not help, for they would not convict British sailors or order them returned. Moreover, Britain had never recognized the right of naturalization contained in the American Constitution, and a brisk trade in fake American birth certificates made the situation worse. The British navy, determined to show its sailors the consequence of desertion, made little effort to observe niceties when boarding American ships to seize deserting sailors, and it often took American sailors as well; perhaps seven thousand were seized from 1790 through the War of 1812. Britain's ability to make these boardings with impunity, because of its vastly superior strength, was seen as a national humiliation to Americans. However, though he had very ably challenged the practice to the British government in 1790, Morris perceived the exigencies of war and told one correspondent that America's proper course was a clear policy that it would defend sailors in its own territorial waters and nowhere else.

The march to war was motivated by more than these provocations, however. Morris perceived that for many people, war with Britain was a pretext for acquiring Canada, which he alleged was tied to the South's ambition to preserve and spread slavery in the West and in Florida. He also believed that the decision to take out loans to pay for the war was a poorly disguised ploy by the South to avoid direct taxes required by the Constitution. Direct taxes would have been burdensome on the slave states, who had benefited from their increased representation in the House under the bitterly contested "three-fifths rule" agreed to at the Constitutional Convention.

Morris's bitter opposition to the war seems to have done much to sully his reputation. Yet there remain legitimate reasons to question the American government's conduct in the years preceding the war. It is sometimes forgotten that in June 1812, as the nation prepared for war, the British, under pressure from their own merchant community, repealed their most offensive measures affecting American trade, leaving only the impressment issue as a basis for war. Nonetheless, when the news arrived in America five weeks later, Madison continued with the war effort.

The decade of Republican diplomatic failure, and an increasing tendency to legislate on the basis of party alignment rather than with regard to the whole nation's welfare, convinced Morris that the Constitution had been abandoned. He believed that the sectional split he had foreseen in his travels in the South—a vast cultural divide between a vigorous commercial North and an aristocracy of Southern gentlemen whose husbandry left their lands enervated—was now at hand. He spoke vigorously against the war and, when many of the disaffected in the North began to talk of severing their states from the South, he joined them. In the summer of 1812 he published a pseudonymous letter in a New York paper advocating secession, calling the war "founded in moral Wrong." The following year, he proposed a meeting of the antiwar states, consisting of New York and the New England states. The meeting took place at the end of 1814 at Hartford, but the resulting resolutions were unsatisfactory to him, and the arrival of the news of the Treaty of Ghent squelched the secessionist movement. Morris accepted this result, and, though he still despised the Madison administration, advised his fellow Federalists to put the war and the secessionist movement behind them.

The last years of Morris's life were marked by physical suffering. He had long endured the misery of gout, a family curse that was a constant companion throughout his wanderings in Europe and revisited him with increasing frequency as he aged. He also had a chronic inflammation of the urethra, first mentioned in his diary in November 1794. Apparently he later attempted to open the obstruction by a failed attempt to operate on himself with a whalebone, which undoubtedly exacerbated the problem. By the summer of 1816 he rarely left his house; whether he knew death was imminent is uncertain, but he described himself as descending "with tottering steps the bottom of life's hill."

He felt well enough, however, to plan to take Anne on a visit to Virginia that fall, and either she or he apparently wrote to Jefferson to propose a stop at Monticello. Jefferson responded on October 16 with warm enthusiasm. He was about to depart Monticello for one of his other properties and told Morris he would "be really mortified" if he missed them:

> I shall be very happy indeed to receive you here and to give you personal assurances of my continued esteem. You will find me enjoying general good health but much enfeebled by age, as at that of 73 ought to be expected. Should I however not be returned, my daughter, your quondam acquaintance in Paris, now surrounded by her children and grandchildren will be happy in the opportunity of renewing old acquaintance with you, and the more as she will be charged to pay to you, as my representative here, the friendly attentions I should so much rather have done myself. . . . With my respects to Mrs. Morris accept the assurance of my great consideration and esteem.
>
> Th. Jefferson

Morris lived for three weeks after Jefferson wrote this letter; perhaps it arrived in time to be read to him. We shall never know what such a visit might have produced in their relationship.

On October 19, Gouverneur Morris made his last diary entry. On November 6, 1816, he died.

"Were I called upon to distinguish him by a single trait," his friend Madame de Damas wrote in her acute verbal portrait of Gouverneur Morris, "I should say, *he is good*." She included "much in the term *goodness*" and saw "the exercise of this virtue in every action of Mr. Morris's life."

This is a unique epitaph for one of our Founding Fathers, and one that deserves reflection. Morris was disliked by many in his own day and continues to draw the contempt of many modern historians. William Howard Adams's subtitle of his scholarly biography of Morris, "An Independent Life," is probably the most succinct explanation of that persistent disregard—Morris had no interest in burnishing his own legend for posterity.

But he was without question a vital Founding Father, one whose skillful, brilliant, and often daring efforts in the cause were indispensable in the Revolution and in the formation of the new nation's Constitution. His beloved manor of Morrisania in the Bronx is unfortunately long gone, razed more than a hundred years ago. There remain no beautiful grounds or elegant house for us to visit. But his vivid presence can still be felt, for Morris comes to life on the page. He was above all a man of words, and his letters, his speeches on the floor of the Constitutional Convention, and most of all his diaries, have preserved his essence.

In 1780, Richard Henry Lee described Morris as a "flutterer on the surface," but the story of his life makes such a judgment seem not just malicious but absurd. This is a man worth getting to know, one who, despite the difficult ordeals he endured, firmly believed in a merciful God for whom "to enjoy is to obey." A humane and honorable man who understood the weaknesses of men and women better than most and did his best to design a government that would uphold liberty while making due provision for human frailty. A man who did not live life cautiously but rather to the full, and in doing so made invaluable and lasting contributions to our country. The example of Gouverneur Morris should continue to instruct and inspire us.

Fig. 8: Gouverneur Morris by Ezra Ames. This is a late portrait of Morris, dating from around 1815, a year before his death at the age of sixty-four.

BIBLIOGRAPHY

For the chapters concerning Morris's ancestors, Morris's youth, and Morris's experiences during the American Revolution, I am indebted to the work of Max Mintz, William Howard Adams, Mary-Jo Kline, and Richard Brookhiser. For my discussion of the Newburgh Conspiracy discussion, I also drew on an article by J. Edward Skeen and Richard H. Kohn. For Morris's contributions to the Constitutional Convention, Arthur Paul Kaufman's excellent review and analysis in his doctoral dissertation, along with frequent consultation of the Avalon Project's wonderful online edition of the debates of the Convention, informed the discussion.

Morris's experiences in France drew on the work I did for my *Envoy to the Terror: Gouverneur Morris and the French Revolution*. For Morris's life after returning to the United States, the books by Mintz, Adams, and Brookhiser were invaluable.

Primary Sources

Published Works

Granville, George, Duke of Sutherland. *The Despatches of Earl Gower.* Edited by Oscar Browning. Cambridge, UK: Cambridge University Press, 1885.

Hamilton, Alexander. *The Papers of Alexander Hamilton.* Edited by Harold C. Syrett et al. 27 vols. New York: Columbia University Press, 1961–87.

Jay, John. *The Winning of the Peace: Unpublished Papers, 1780–1784.* Edited by Richard B. Morris. New York: Harper & Row, 1980.

Jefferson, Thomas. *The Papers of Thomas Jefferson.* Edited by Julian Boyd, Charles T. Cullen, John Catanzariti, and Barbara B. Oberg. Princeton, NJ: Princeton University Press, 1950– .

Lafayette, Marie Joseph Paul Yves Roch Gilbert Du Motier, Marquis de. *Mémoires, Correspondance et manuscrits du Général Lafayette.* Edited by H. Fournier Aîné. London: Saunders & Otley, 1837.

Lally-Tolendal, Trophime-Gérard, Marquis de. *Mémoire de Lally-Tolendal, au roi de Prusse, pour réclamer la liberté de Lafayette.* Paris: Chez les marchands de nouveautés, 1795.

Le Patriote Français, journal libre, impartial et national; Par une Société de citoyens, et dirigée par J. P. Brissot de Warville. 8 vols. Frankfurt am Main: Keip Verlag, 1989.

Lee, Richard Henry, *The Letters of Richard Henry Lee.* Edited by James Curtis Ballagh. 2 vols. New York: Macmillan, 1914.

Letters of Delegates to Congress, 1774–1789, Volume 15, April 1, 1780–August 31, 1780. Edited by Paul H. Smith, et al. Washington, D.C.: Library of Congress, 1976–2000.

Maclay, William. *The Journal of William Maclay, United States Senator from Pennsylvania, 1789–1791.* New York: Albert and Charles Boni, 1927.

Madison, James. *Letters and Other Writings of James Madison.* 4 vols. Philadelphia: J. B. Lippincott, 1865.

Mallet du Pan, Jacques. *Memoirs and Correspondence of Mallet du Pan.* Edited by A. Sayous. 2 vols. London: R. Bentley, 1852.

Malouet, Pierre-Victor. *Mémoires de Malouet.* 2 vols. Paris: E. Plon, 1874.

Manuscripts of J. B. Fortescue, Esq., Preserved at Dropmore, Vol. 2. Historical

Manuscripts Commission, Fourteenth Report (vol. 14), pt. 5. London: Eyre and Spottiswood, 1894.

Miranda, Francisco de. *Archivo del general Miranda.* 24 vols. Caracas: Editorial Sur-América, 1929–50.

Moleville, Bertrand de. *Private Memoirs Relative to the Last Year of the Reign of Louis the Sixteenth.* 3 vols. London: printed for A. Strahan, T. Cadell, and W. Davies, 1797.

Morris, Gouverneur. *A Diary of the French Revolution.* Edited by Beatrix Cary Davenport. 2 vols. Boston: Houghton Mifflin, 1939.

————. *The Diary and Letters of Gouverneur Morris.* Edited by Anne Cary Morris. 2 vols. New York: Scribner's, 1888.

Morris, Lewis. *The Papers of Lewis Morris,* Vol. 1, edited by Eugene R. Sheridan. Newark, NJ: Collections of the New Jersey Historical Society, no. 24, 1991

Paine, Thomas. *The Complete Writings of Thomas Paine.* Edited by Philip S. Foner. 2 vols. New York: Citadel Press, 1945.

————. *The Writings of Thomas Paine.* Edited by Moncure Conway. 4 vols. New York: Putnam, 1895.

Sparks, Jared. *The Life and Correspondence of Gouverneur Morris.* 3 vols. Boston: Gray and Bowen, 1832.

Turner, Frederick Jackson, ed. *Correspondence of the French Ministers to the United States, 1791–1797.* American Historical Society Annual Report (1903).

Washington, George. *The Diaries of George Washington.* Edited by Donald Jackson and Dorothy Twohig. 6 vols. Charlottesville, VA: University Press of Virginia, 1979.

————. *The Papers of George Washington: Confederation Series.* Edited by W. W. Abbot and Dorothy Twohig. 6 vols. Charlottesville, VA: University Press of Virginia, 1992–97.

————. *The Papers of George Washington: The Journal of the Proceedings of the President, 1793–1797.* Edited by Dorothy Twohig. Charlottesville, VA: University Press of Virginia, 1981.

————. *The Papers of George Washington: Presidential Series.* Edited by W. W. Abbot, Dorothy Twohig, and Philander Chase. 11 vols. Charlottesville, VA: University Press of Virginia, 1987–2002.

Unpublished Works

Archives du Ministère des Affaires Étrangères, États-Unis. Foreign Copying Project, France, Manuscripts Division, Library of Congress.

Constable-Pierrepont Papers, New York Public Library.

Knox Papers, Gilder-Lehrman Collection, New York Historical Society.

Monroe, James, Papers, Tracy W. McGregor Library, University of Virginia.

Morris, Gouverneur, Papers, Special Collections, Columbia University Library.

Morris, Gouverneur, Papers, including Commercial Letters, Consular Letterbook, Diary in full, Miscellaneous Papers, Official Letterbook, Private Letterbook, and Waste Book. Manuscripts Division, Library of Congress.

Morris Family Papers, New York Historical Society.

Pinckney Family Papers, Manuscripts Division, Library of Congress.

Shippen Family Papers, Manuscripts Division, Library of Congress.

Smith Family Papers, Series 41—Gouverneur Morris, American Philosophical Society, Philadelphia.

Secondary Sources

Books

Adams, William Howard. *Gouverneur Morris: An Independent Life.* New Haven, CT: Yale University Press, 2003.

Alden, John R. *Stephen Sayre, American Revolutionary Adventurer.* Baton Rouge, LA: Louisiana State University Press, 1983.

Boyd, Julian. *Number 7—Alexander Hamilton's Secret Attempts to Control American Foreign Policy.* Princeton, NJ: Princeton University Press, 1964.

Brookhiser, Richard. *Gentleman Revolutionary: Gouverneur Morris—The Rake Who Wrote the Constitution.* New York: Free Press, 2003.

Chernow, Barbara Ann. *Robert Morris, Land Speculator 1790–1801.* Dissertations in American Economic History. New York: Arno Press, 1978.

Crawford, Alan Pell. *Unwise Passions: A True Story of a Remarkable Woman and the First Great Scandal of Eighteenth-Century America.* New York: Simon & Schuster, 2000.

DeConde, Alexander. *Entangling Alliance: Politics and Diplomacy under George Washington.* Durham, NC: Duke University Press, 1958.

Ellery, Eloise. *Brissot de Warville.* Boston: Houghton Mifflin, 1915.

Fiechter, Jean-Jacques. *Un diplomate américain sous la Terreur: Les années européennes de Gouverneur Morris, 1789–1798.* Paris: Fayard, 1983.

Furet, François, and Monica Ouzouf, eds. *A Critical Dictionary of the French Revolution.* Cambridge, MA: Belknap Press, 1989.

Furet, François, and Denis Richet. *French Revolution.* Translated by Stephen Hardman. New York: MacMillan, 1970.

Gottschalk, Louis, and Margaret Maddox. *Lafayette in the French Revolution: From the October Days through the Federation.* Chicago: University of Chicago Press, 1973.

Hardman, John. *Louis XVI.* New Haven, CT: Yale University Press, 1993.

Harris, Robert. *Necker: Reform Statesman of the Ancien Régime.* Berkeley, CA: University of California Press, 1979.

Johnson, Odai, William Burling, and James Coombs. *The Colonial American Stage, 1665–1774: A Documentary Calendar.* Madison, NJ: Fairleigh Dickinson University Press, 2002.

Kaufman, Arthur Paul. *The Constitutional Views of Gouverneur Morris.* Ann Arbor, MI: University of Michigan Dissertation Services, 1994.

Kierner, Cynthia A. *Scandal at Bizarre: Rumor and Reputation in Jefferson's America.* New York: Palgrave MacMillan, 2004.

Kline, Mary-Jo. *Gouverneur Morris and the New Nation: 1775–1788.* New York: Arno Press, 1978.

Miller, Melanie Randolph. *Gouverneur Morris and the French Revolution.* Ann Arbor, MI: University of Michigan Dissertation Services, 2000. Note: this is a six-hundred-page version of the published book about Morris's time in France and contains considerably more research and information.

———. *Envoy to the Terror: Gouverneur Morris and the French Revolution.* Dulles, VA: Potomac Books, 2004.

Mintz, Maxwell. *Gouverneur Morris and the American Revolution.* Norman, OK: University of Oklahoma Press, 1970.

Morgan, Edmund S. *The Stamp Act Crisis.* Chapel Hill, NC: University of North Carolina Press, 1995.

O'Brien, Conor Cruise. *The Long Affair: Thomas Jefferson and the French Revolution, 1785–1800.* Chicago: University of Chicago Press, 1996.

Palmer, R. R. *Twelve Who Ruled: The Year of the Terror in the French Revolution.* Princeton, NJ: Princeton University Press, 1941.

Price, Jacob M. *France and the Chesapeake: A History of the French Tobacco Monopoly, 1674–1791, and of Its Relationship to the British and American Tobacco Trades.* 2 vols. Ann Arbor, MI: University of Michigan Press, 1973.

Rakove, Jack. *Original Meanings: Politics and Ideas in the Making of the Constitution.* New York: A. A. Knopf, 1996.

Reinhard, Marcel. *La chute de la royauté.* Paris: Gaillimard, 1969.

Reuter, Frank. *Trials and Triumphs: George Washington's Foreign Policy.* Fort Worth, TX: Texas Christian University Press, 1983.

Roosevelt, Theodore. *Gouverneur Morris.* Cambridge: Houghton Mifflin, 1898.

Shackelford, George Green. *Jefferson's Adoptive Son: the Life of William Short, 1759–1848.* Lexington, KY: University Press of Kentucky, 1993.

Soboul, Albert. *Dictionnaire historique de la révolution française.* Paris: Presses Universitaires de France, 1989.

Swiggett, Howard. *The Extraordinary Mr. Morris.* New York: Doubleday, 1952.

Tackett, Timothy. *Becoming a Revolutionary: The Deputies of the French National Assembly and the Emergence of a Revolutionary Culture.* Princeton, NJ: Princeton University Press, 1996.

de Vallière, Paul. *Le 10 août 1792.* Lausanne: Éditions de l'age d'Homme, 1992.

Ver Steeg, Wick, Daniel Lewis. *A Conspiracy of Well-Intentioned Men: The Society of Thirty and the French Revolution.* New York: Garland, 1987.

Winock, Michel. *L'échec au roi: 1791–1792.* Paris: Olivier Orban, 1991.

Woodress, James. *A Yankee's Odyssey: The Life of Joel Barlow.* Philadelphia: Lippincott Co., 1958.

Unpublished dissertations

Tailby, Donald G. "Chapters in the Business Career of William Constable." Ph.D diss., Rutgers University, 1961.

Articles

Kwass, Michael. "A Kingdom of Taxpayers: State Formation, Privilege, and Political Culture in Eighteenth-Century France." *Journal of Modern History* 70 (1998): 295–339.

Levermore, Charles. "The Whigs of Colonial New York." *American Historical Review* 1 (January 1896): 238–50.

Munger, Jeffrey H. "James Swan and Gouverneur Morris: A Taste for the Ancien Régime in 18th Century America." *The Brazos Forum Review,* 11th meeting, 1995. Waco, TX: Brazos Forum, 1996.

Pingaud, L. "Terrier de Monciel." *Le Correspondant* (August 1879): 577–611.

Rappaport, George David. "The First Description of the Bank of North America." *The William and Mary Quarterly, Third Series* 33 (October 1976): 661–67.

Rice, Howard C. "James Swan: Agent of the French Republic, 1794–1796." *New England Quarterly* 10 (1937): 464–86.

Schreider, Louis, III. "Gouverneur Morris, Connoisseur of French Art." *Apollo* (June 1971): 470–83.

Skeen, J. Edward, and Richard H. Kohn. "The Newburgh Conspiracy Reconsidered." *The William and Mary Quarterly, Third Series* 31 (April 1974): 273–98.

Sparrow, Elizabeth, and Paul Penzance. "Secret Service Under Pitt's Administrations." *History* 83 (April 1998): 280–94.

INDEX

ABOUT THE AUTHOR

Melanie Randolph Miller began her professional career in aeronautical engineering before going on to law school and finally obtaining a doctorate in American history. She is the editor of the Gouverneur Morris Papers: Diaries Project and the author of *Envoy to the Terror: Gouverneur Morris and the French Revolution.*